MEN Volume 2

www.dsimoneauphoto.com   (general photography)
www.point-of-view-imagery.com   (male figurative photography)

Photography by Dan Simoneau

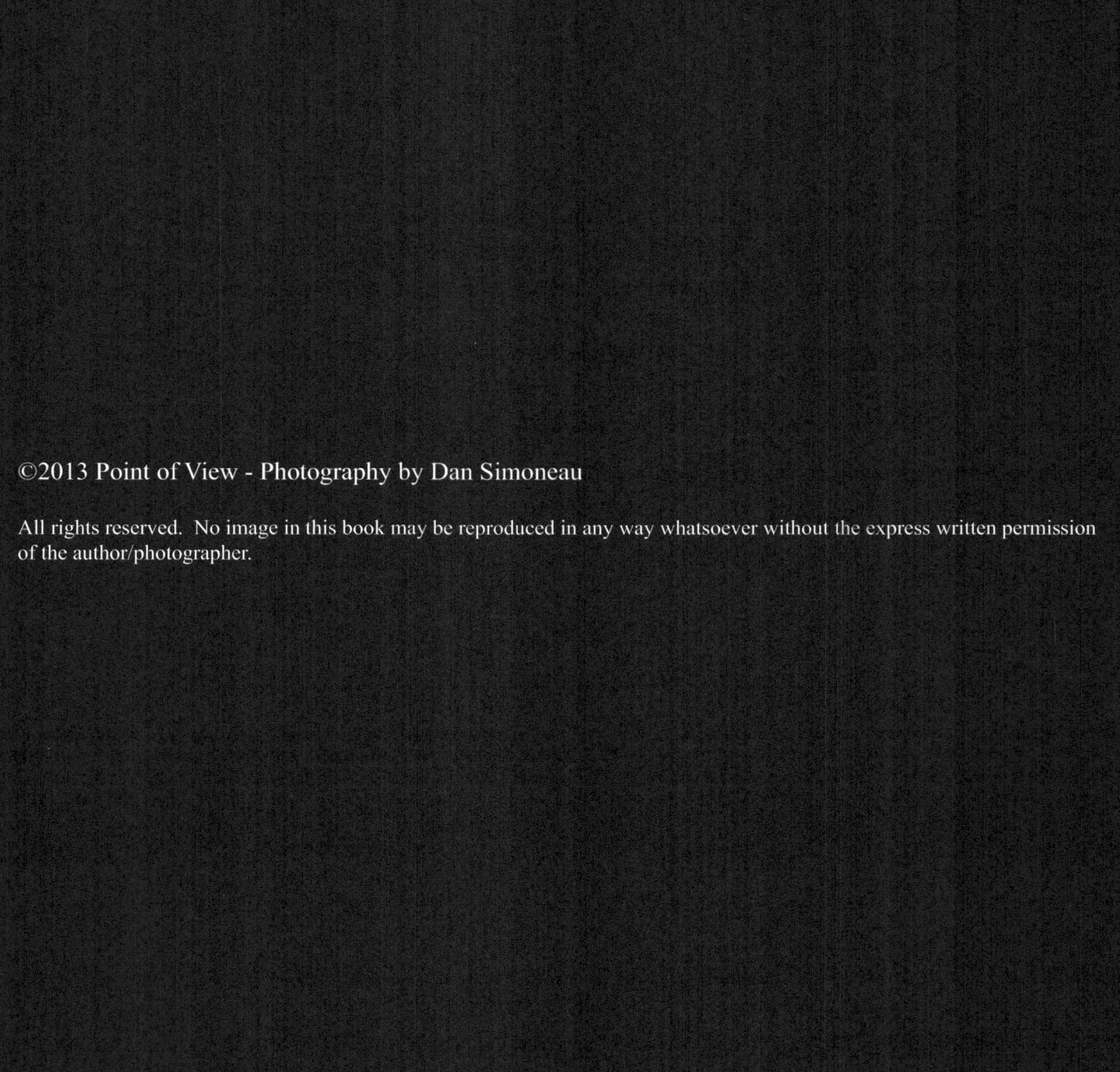

Welcome to volume 2 of my Men series. In volume 1, you met the following men:

Evertz Saenz (Evy)
Rafael Vasquez (Raffy)
Quincey Whittington
Walter Rhone (Dubya Starr)
Scott Vayo
Jake Brennen
Marco Moxie
Michael Dixon

In volume 2 let me introduce you to the following men:

Patrick Galten
Shawn Clayton
Prince Pop
Adonai Dax
Devon Gregory
Monroe Stevens

Thanks to all of my models for working with me to create the images you'll see in both volumes. Also, thank you to Model Mayhem (www.modelmayhem.com) for connecting me to the majority of the models I've worked with.

If you are interested in purchasing signed prints from either book, please contact me through my website, www.point-of-view-imagery.com, letting me know the volume, the model, and page of each image you're interested in. Pricing and sizes can be seen on the website via the purchase gallery.

Thank you for your support.

Dan Simoneau
Point of View - Imagery by Dan Simoneau

Patrick

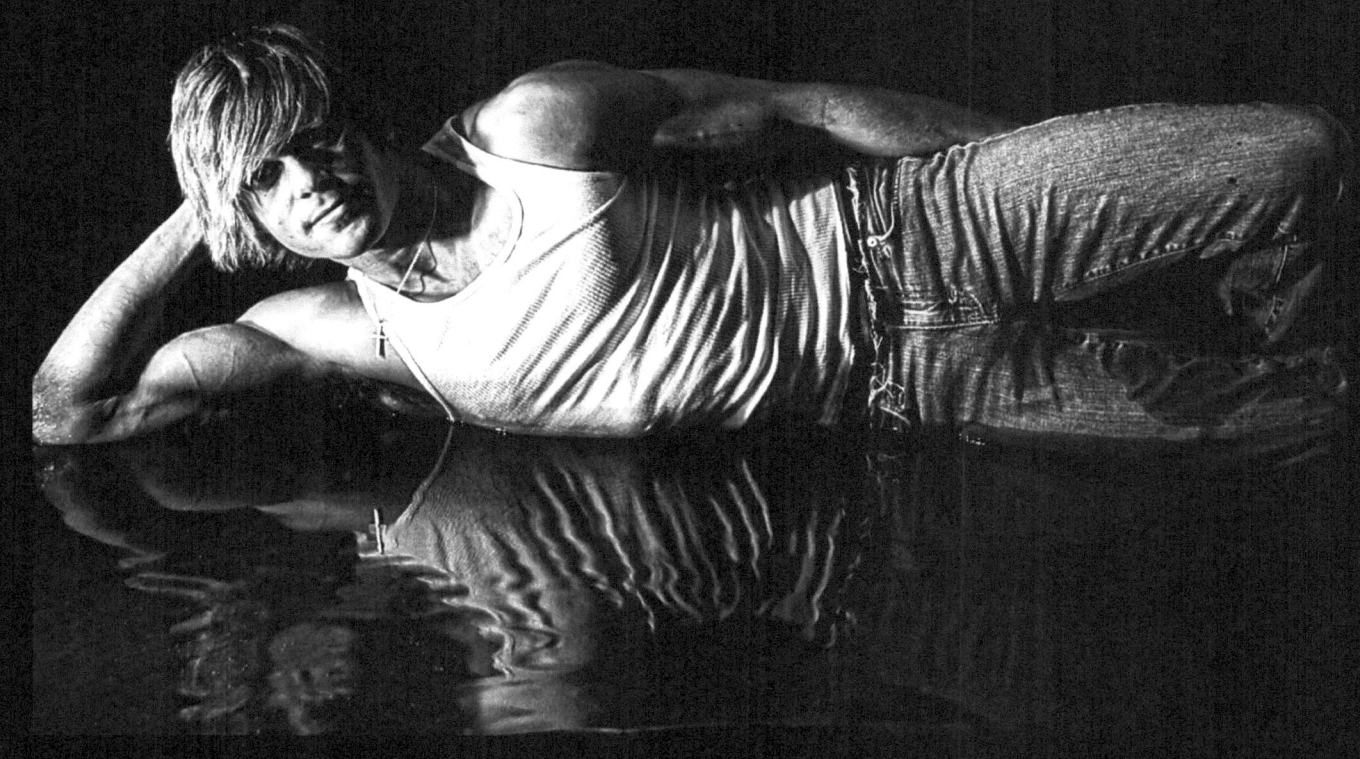

Printed in U.S.A

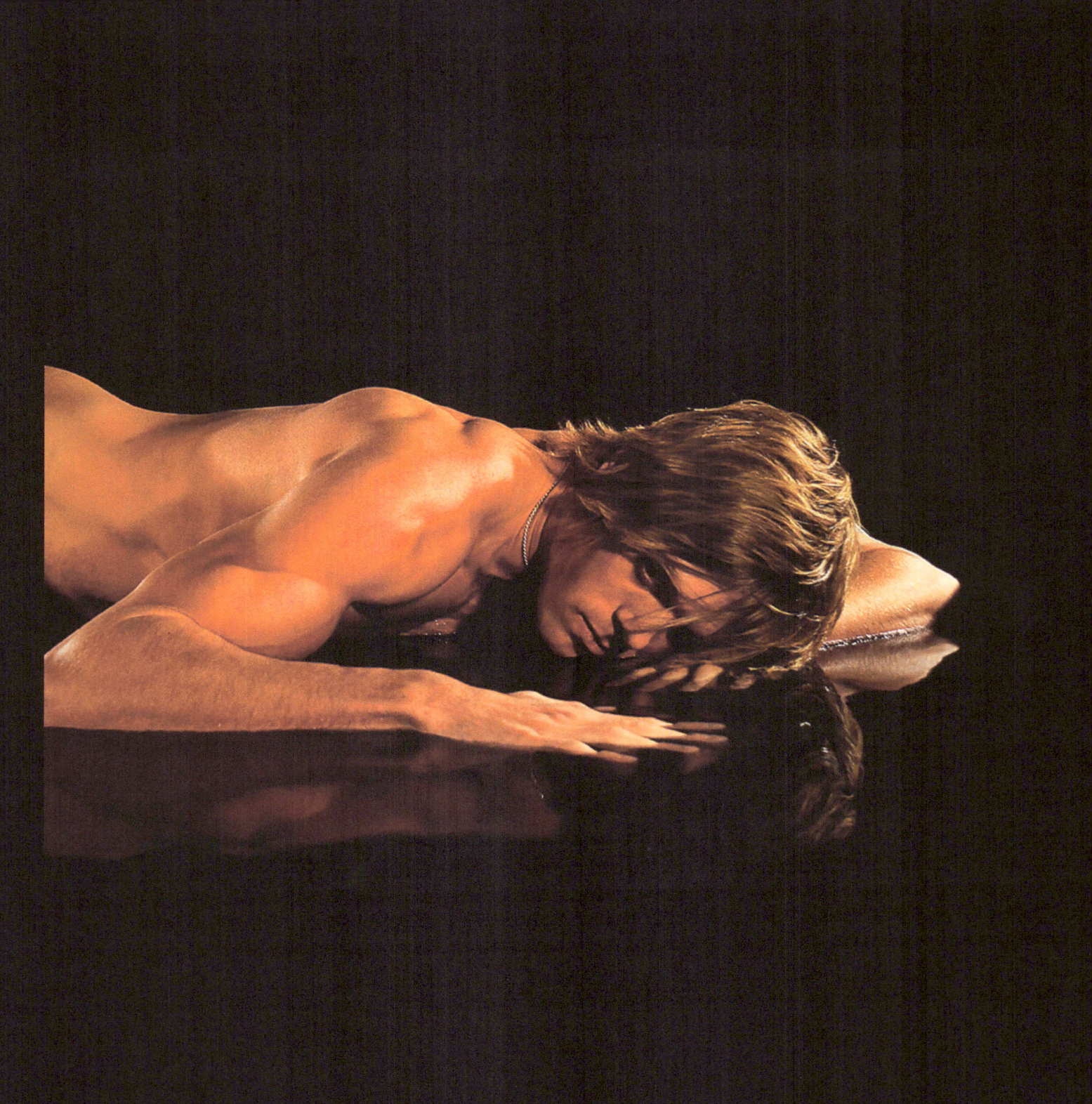

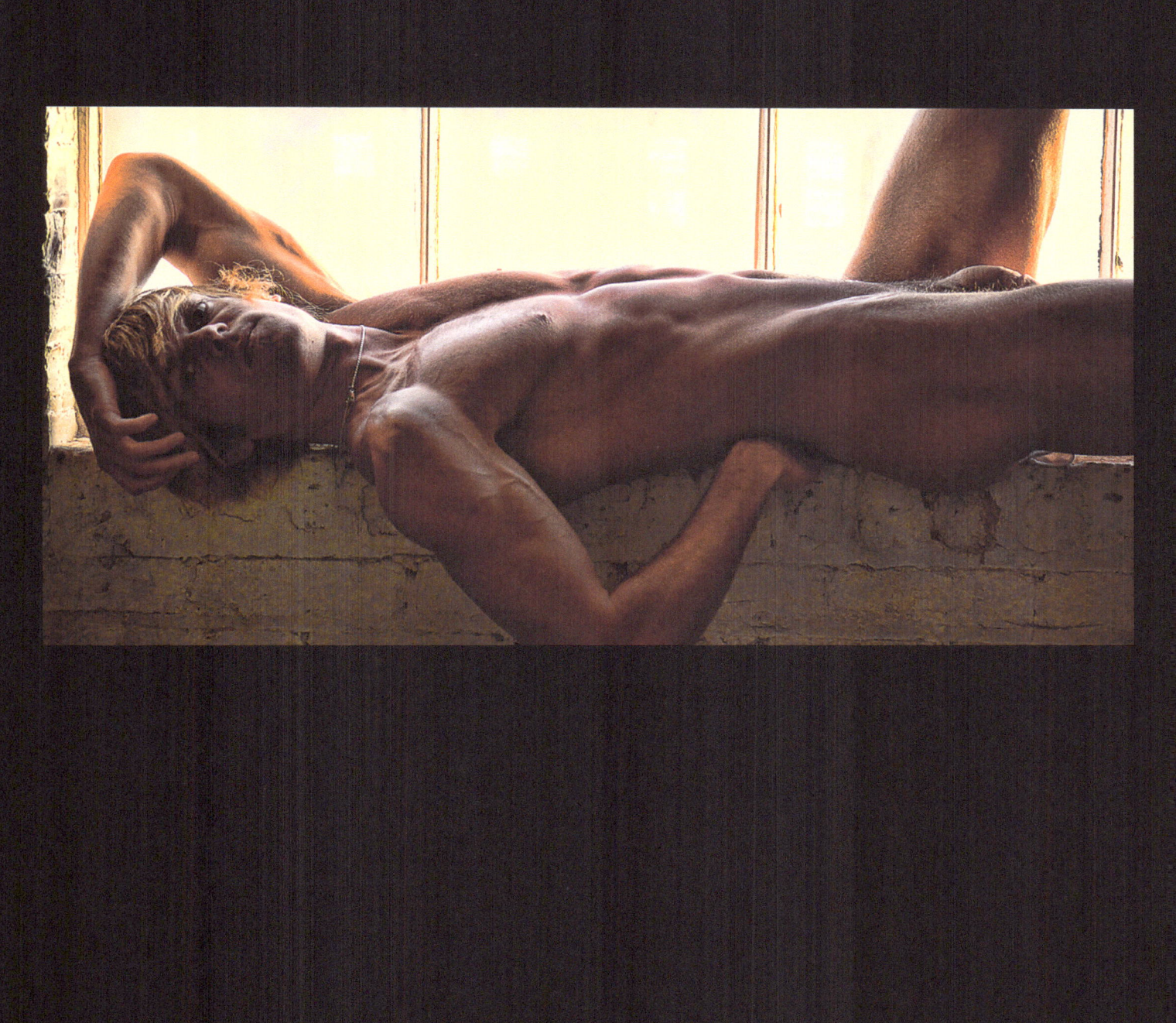

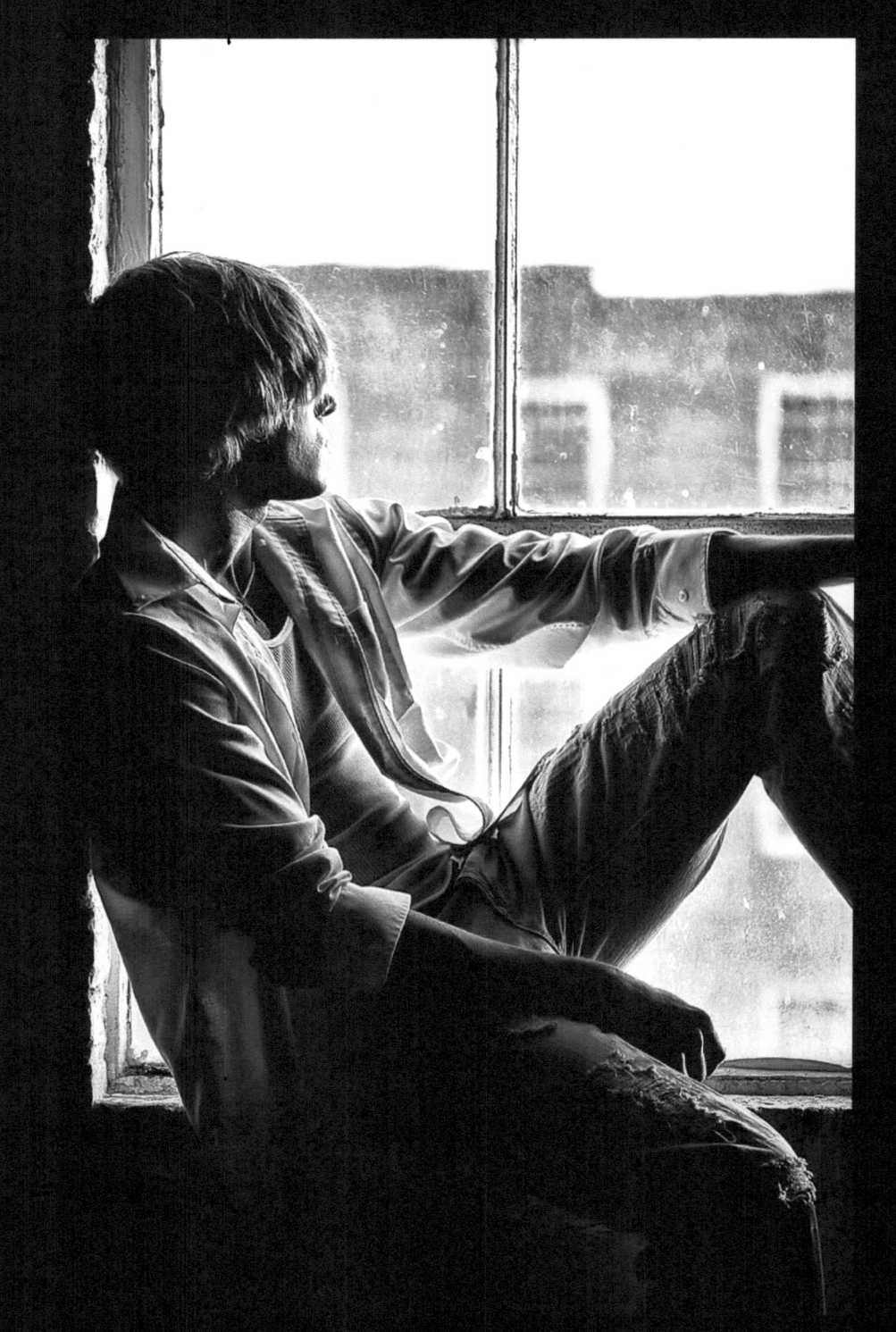

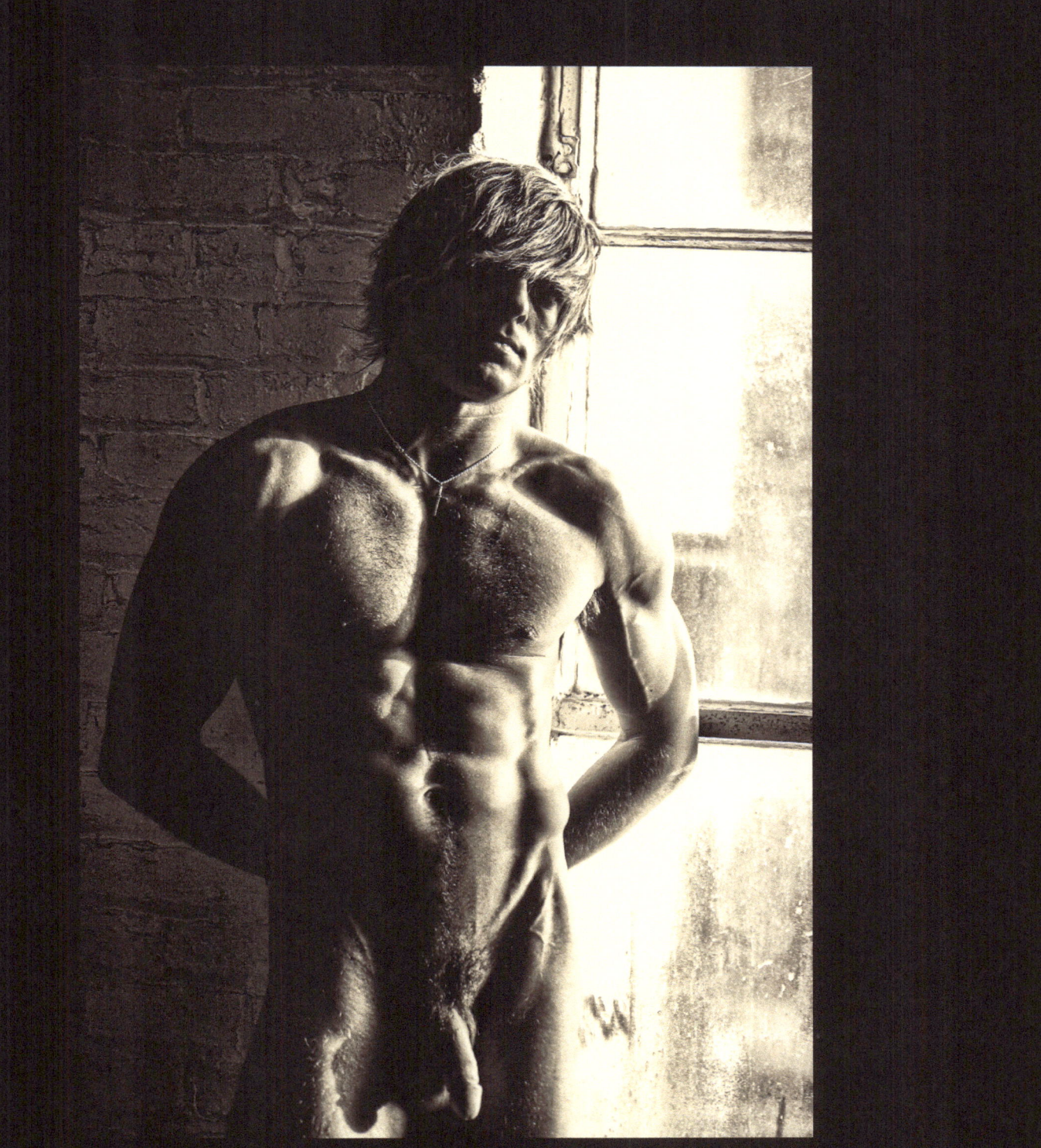

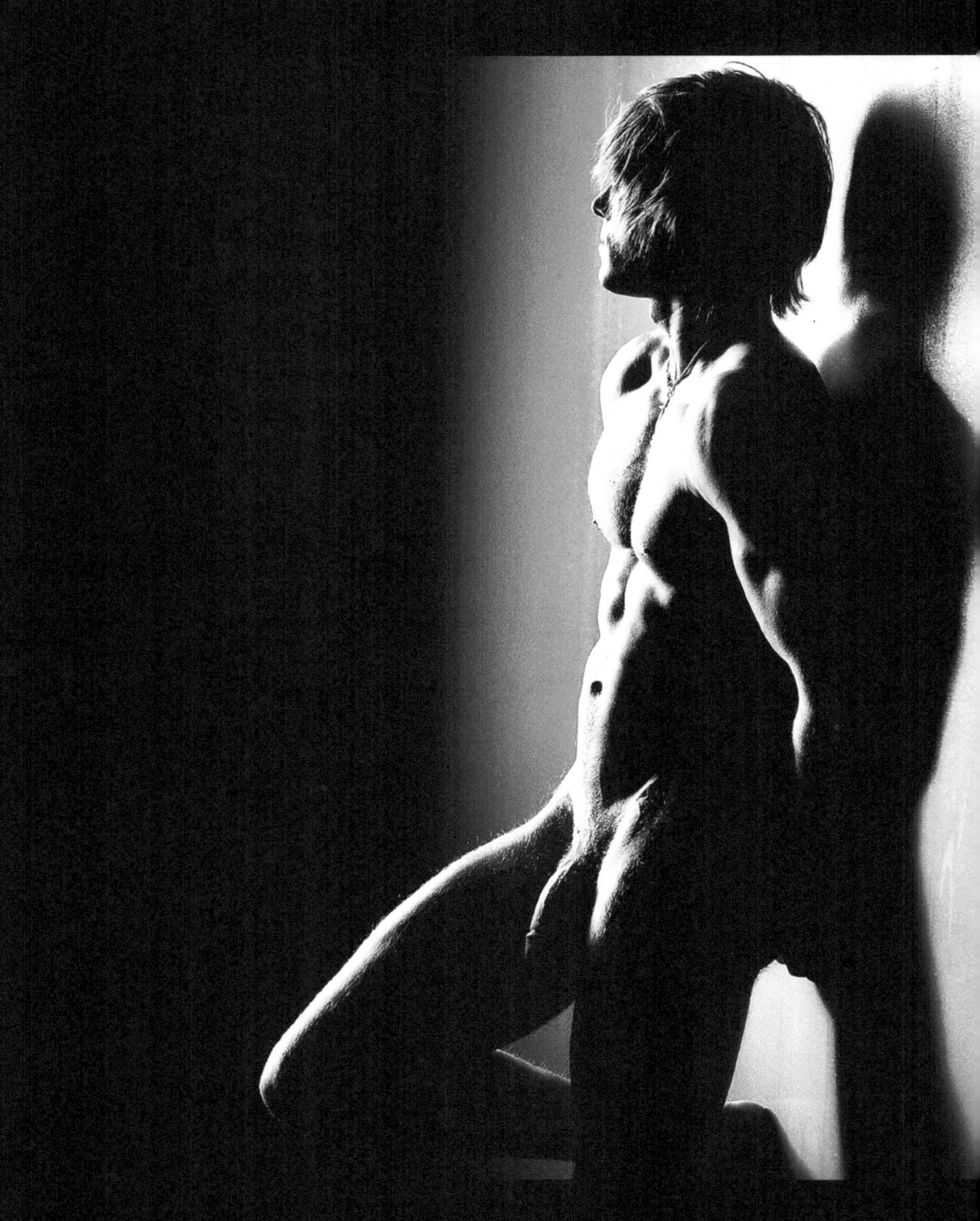

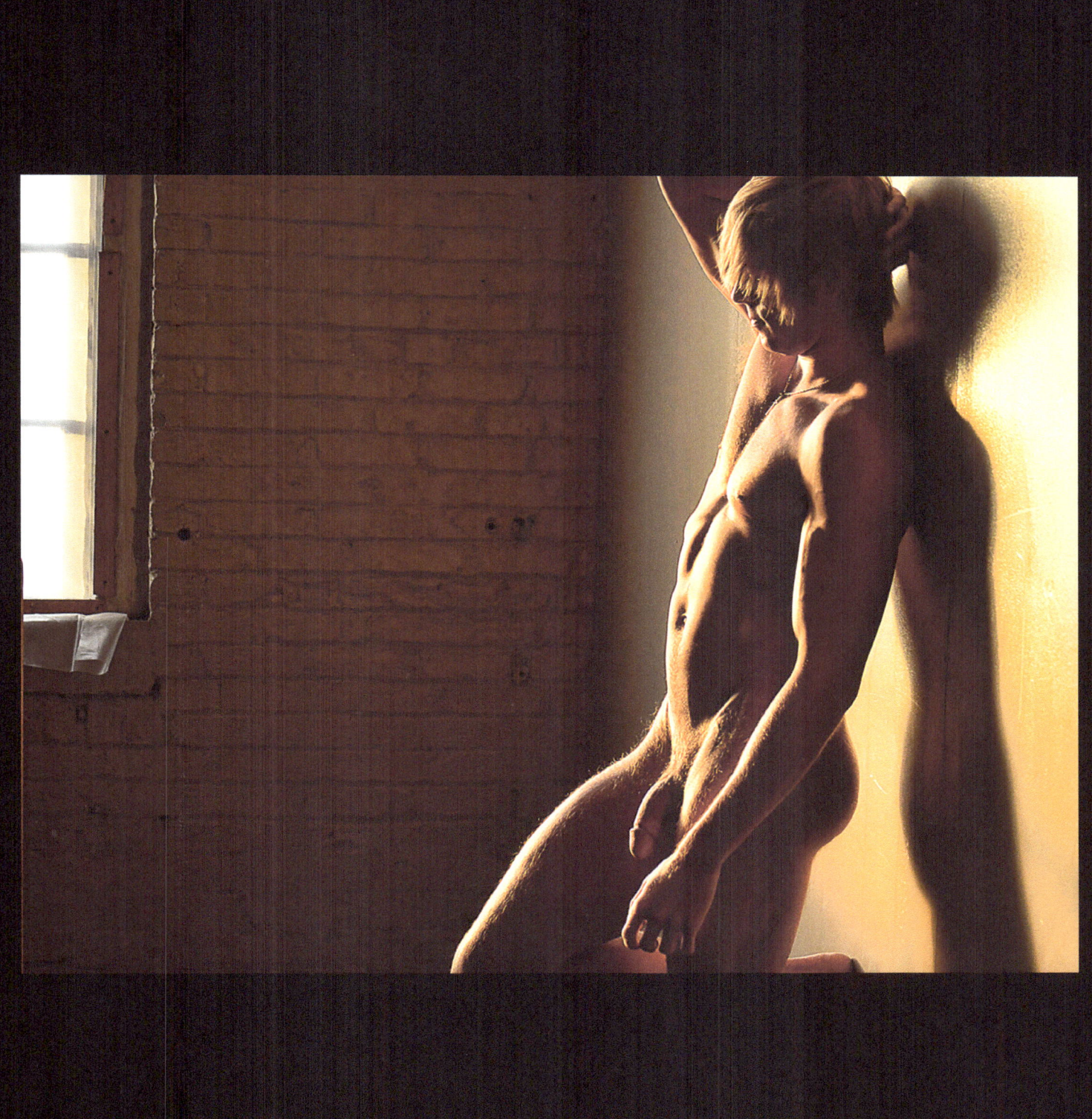

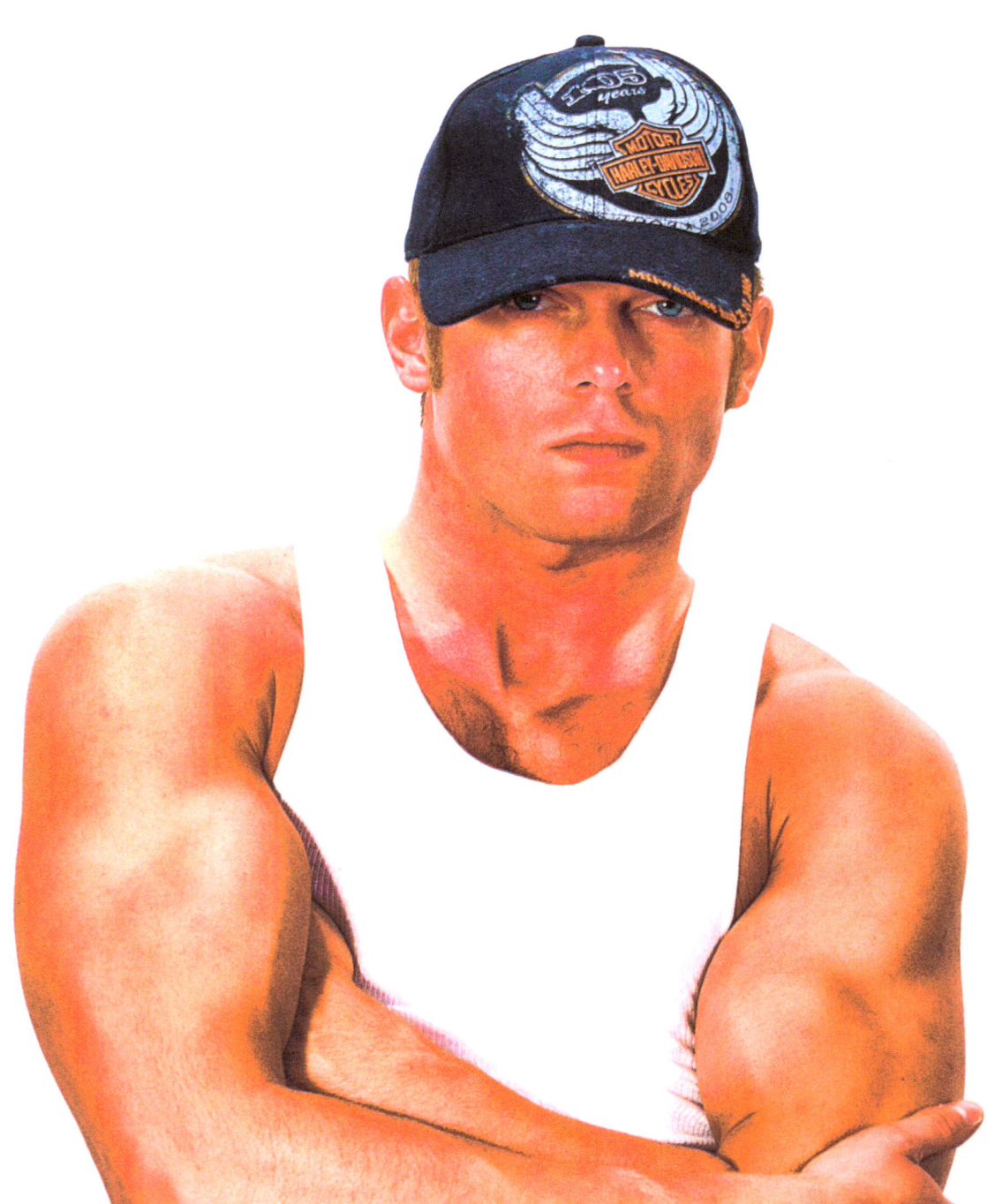

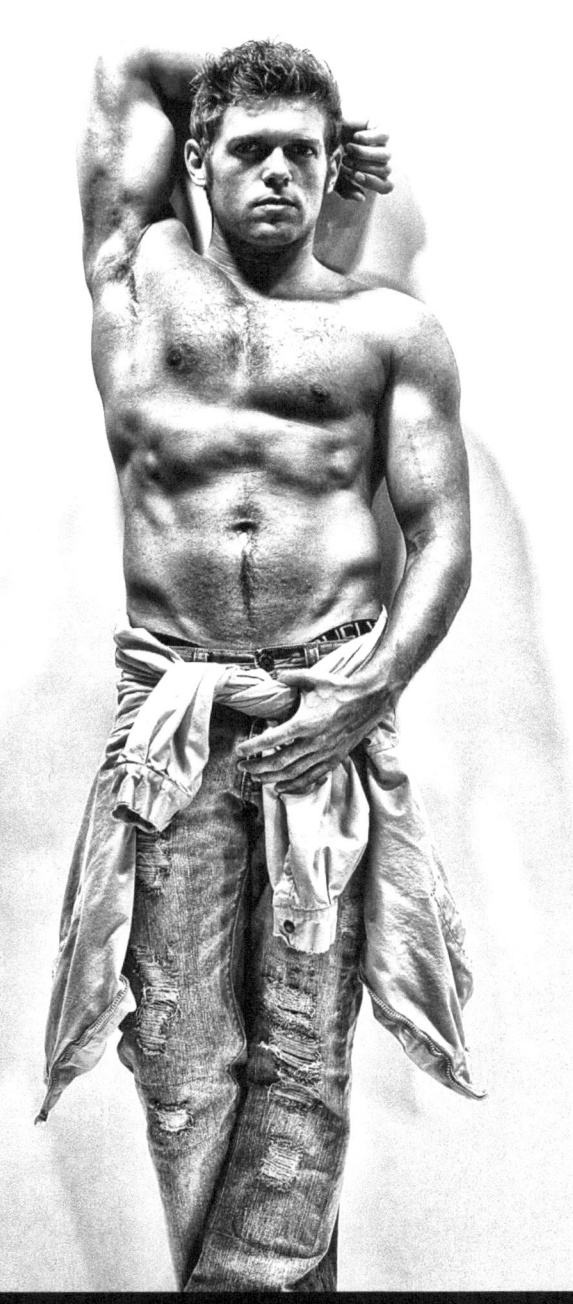

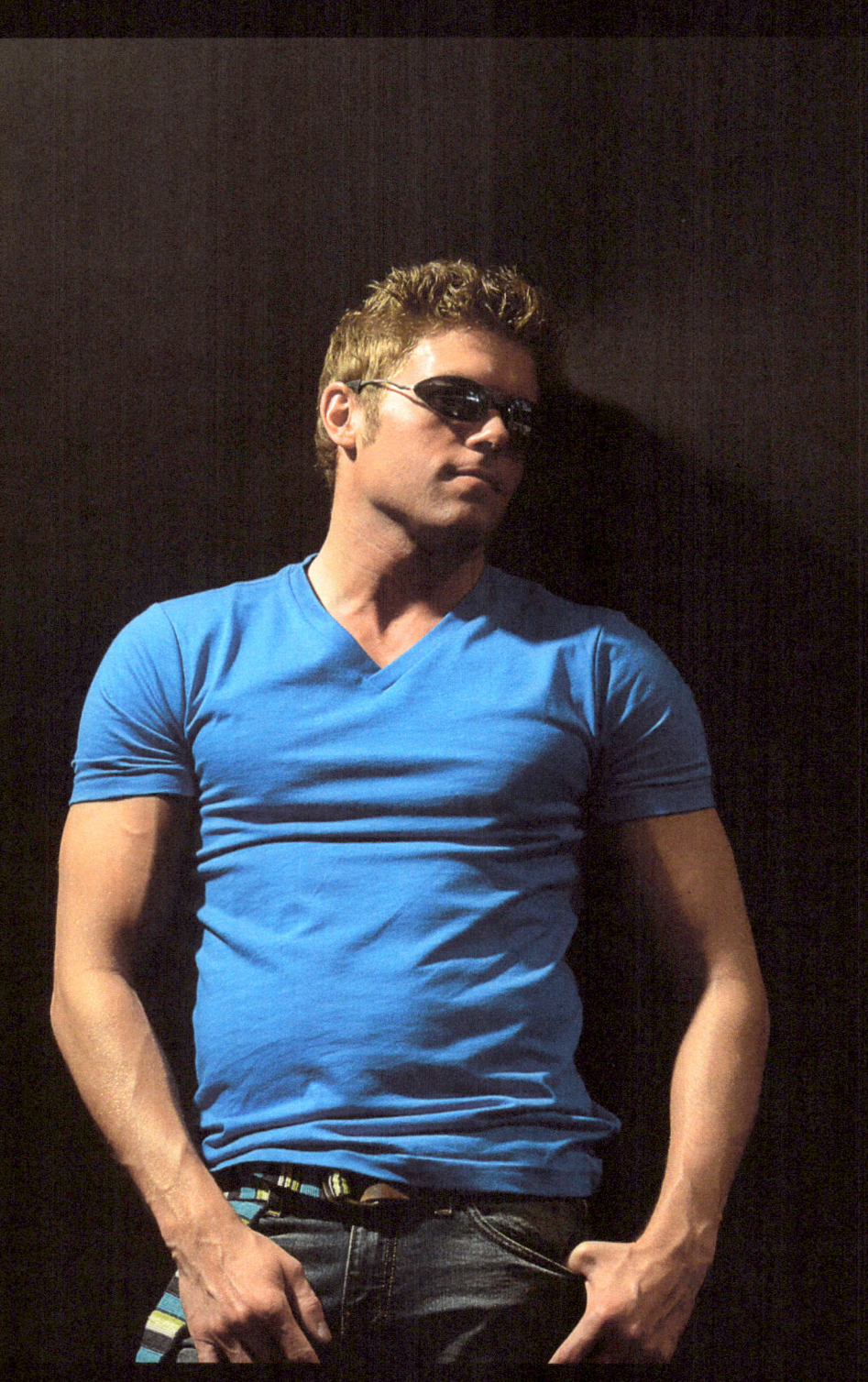

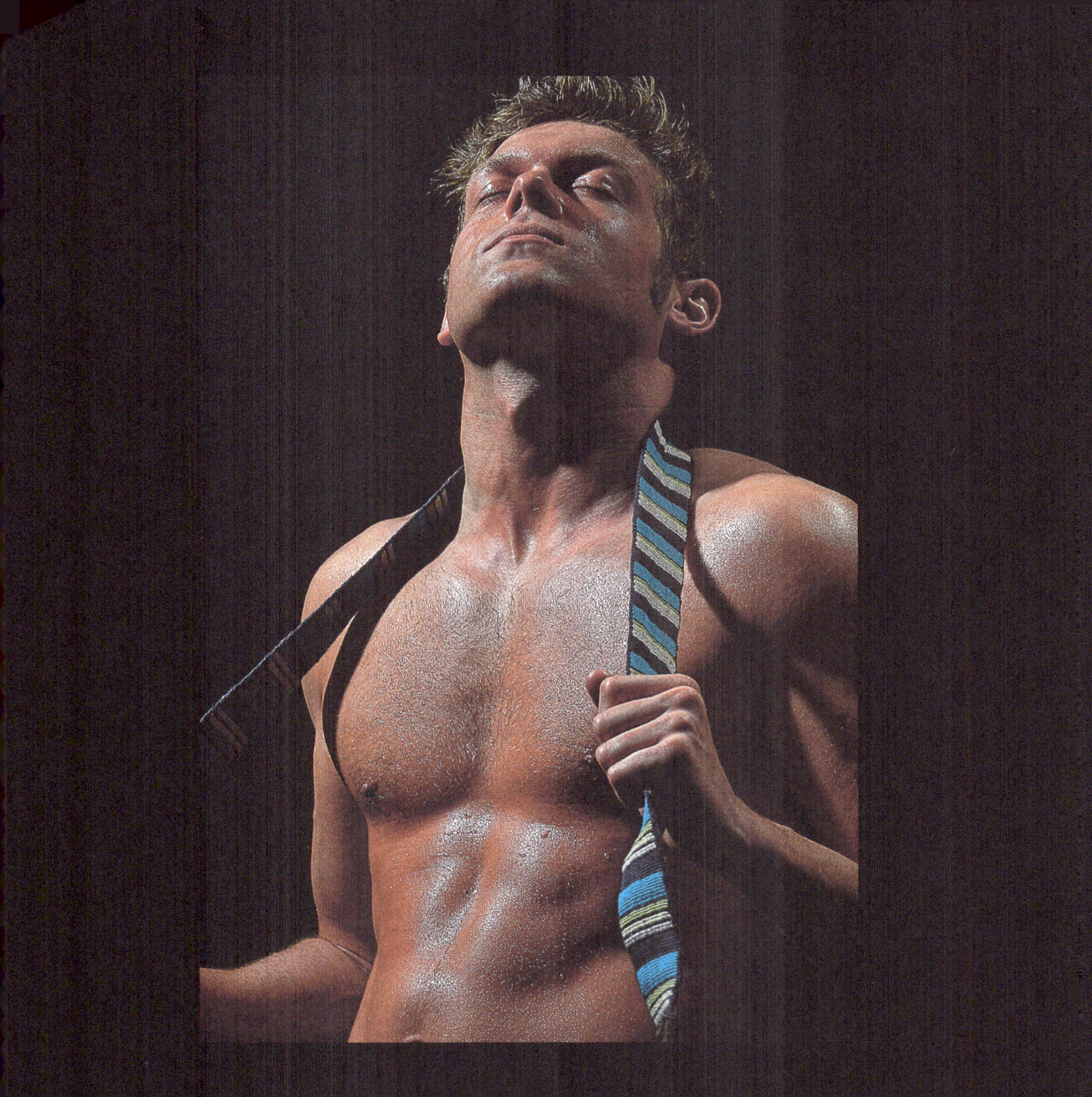

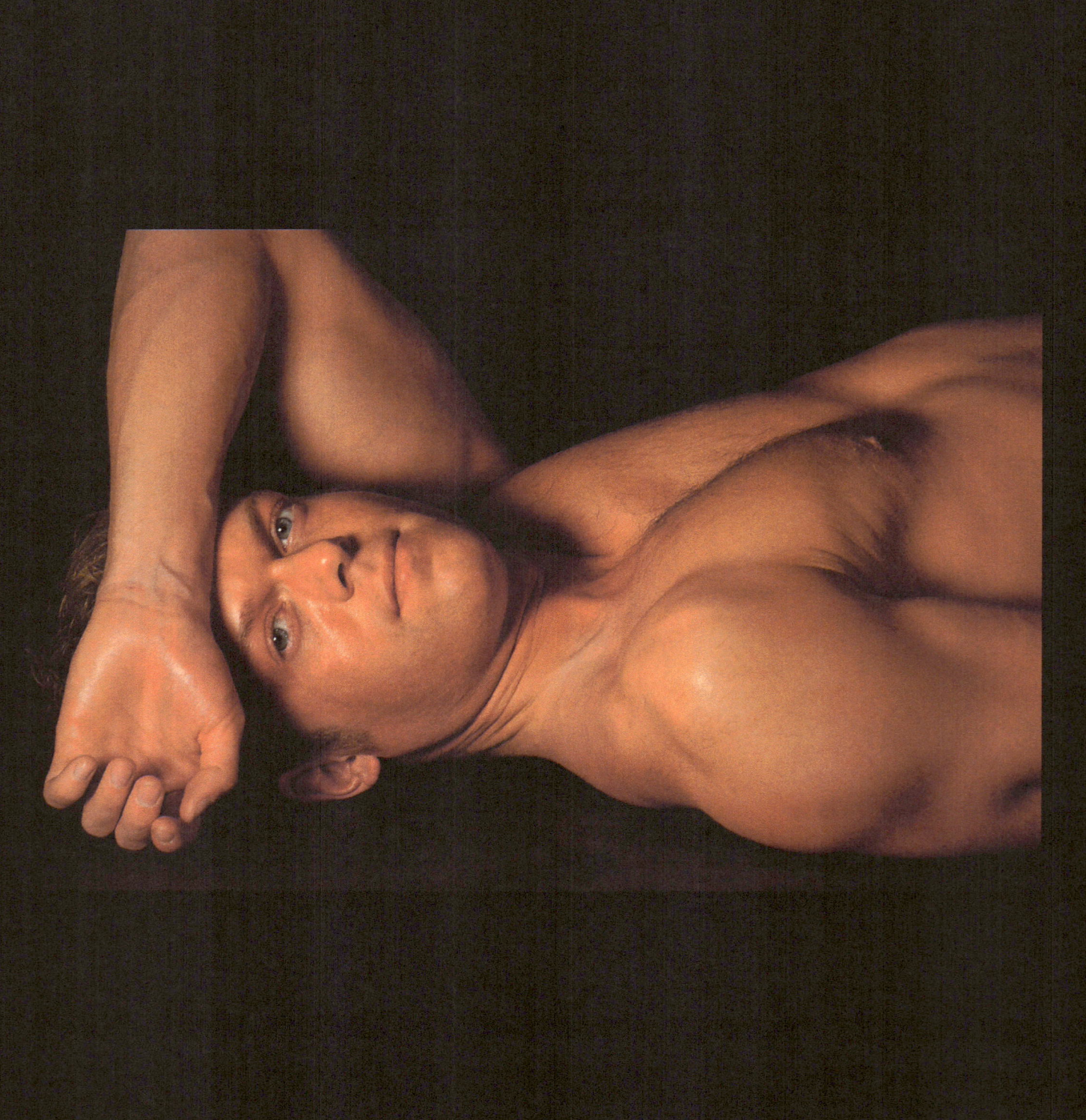

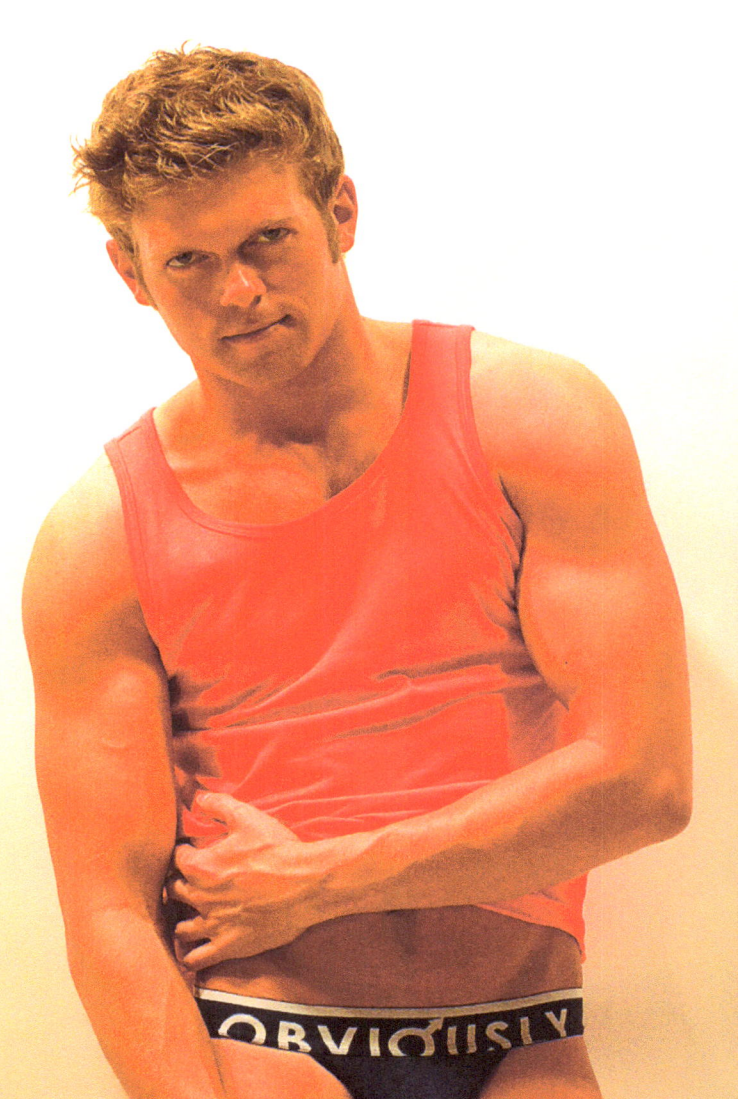

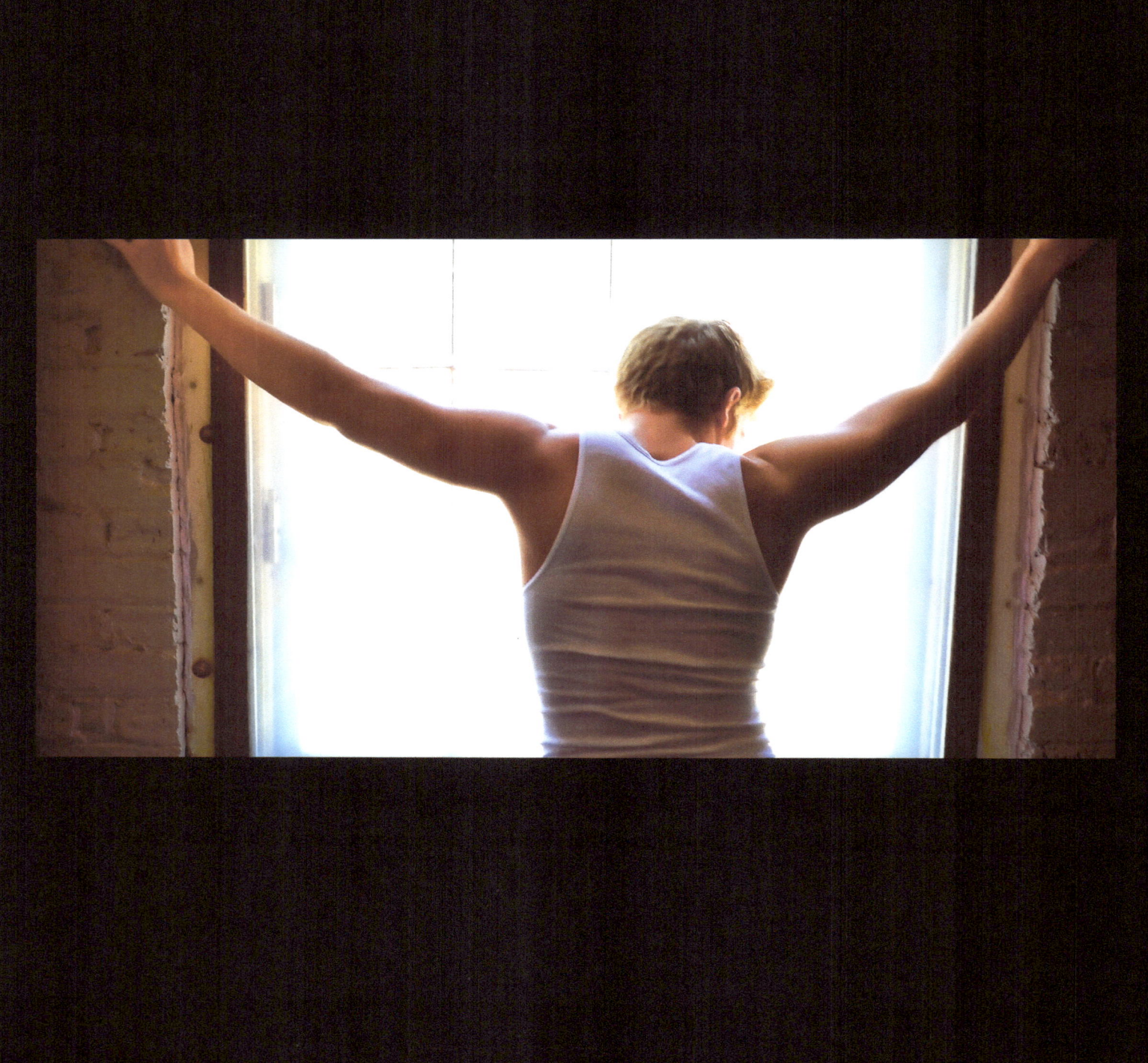

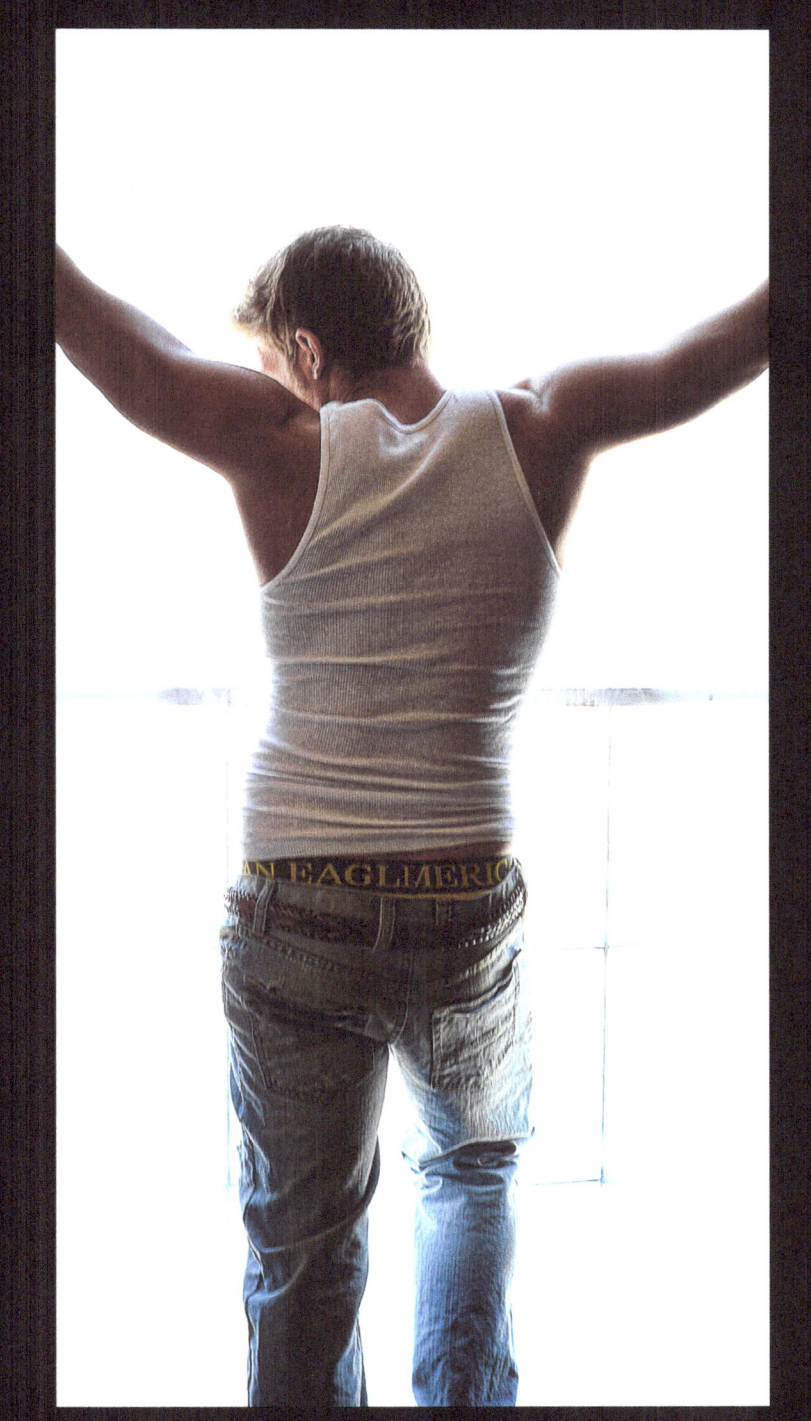

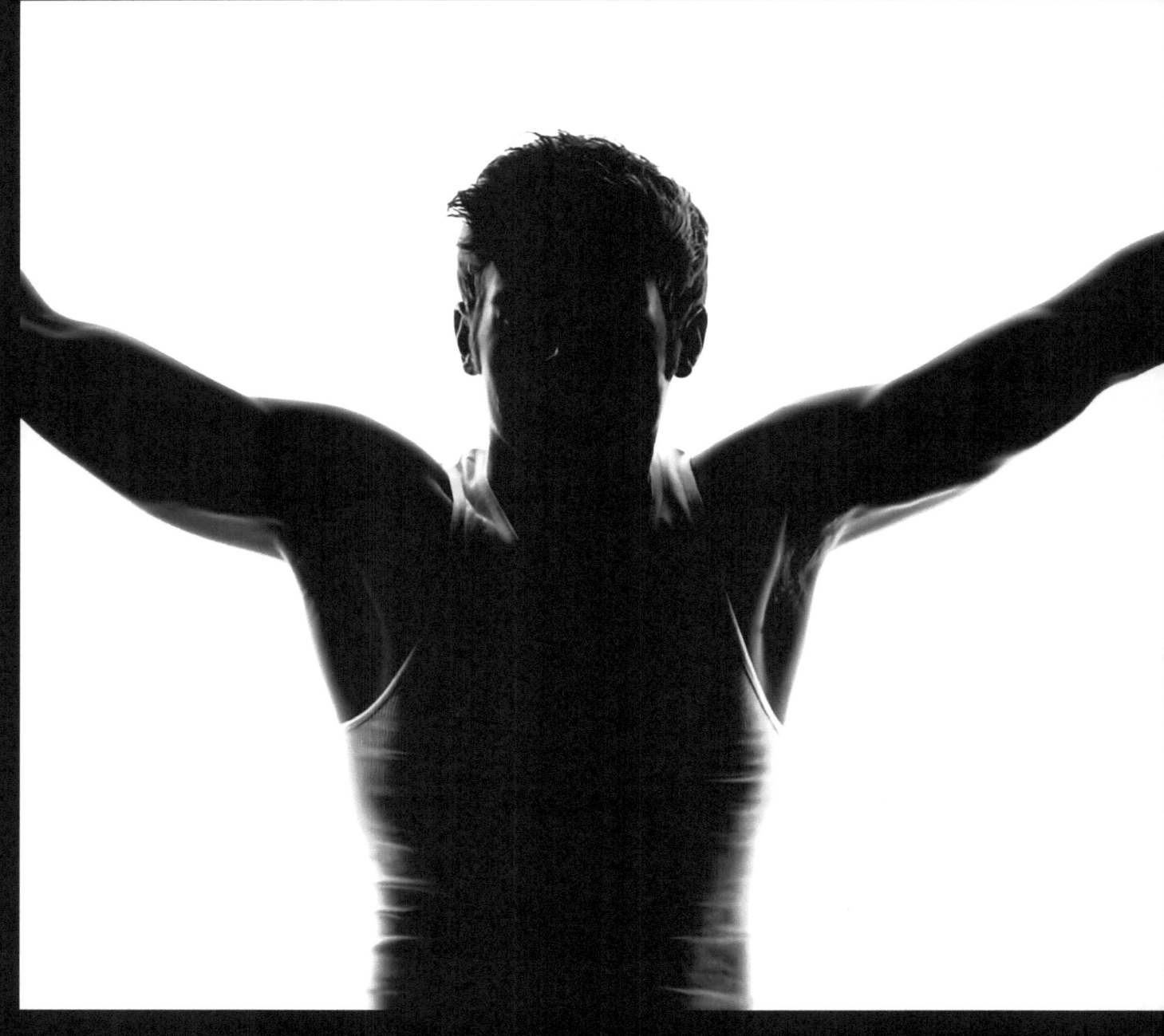

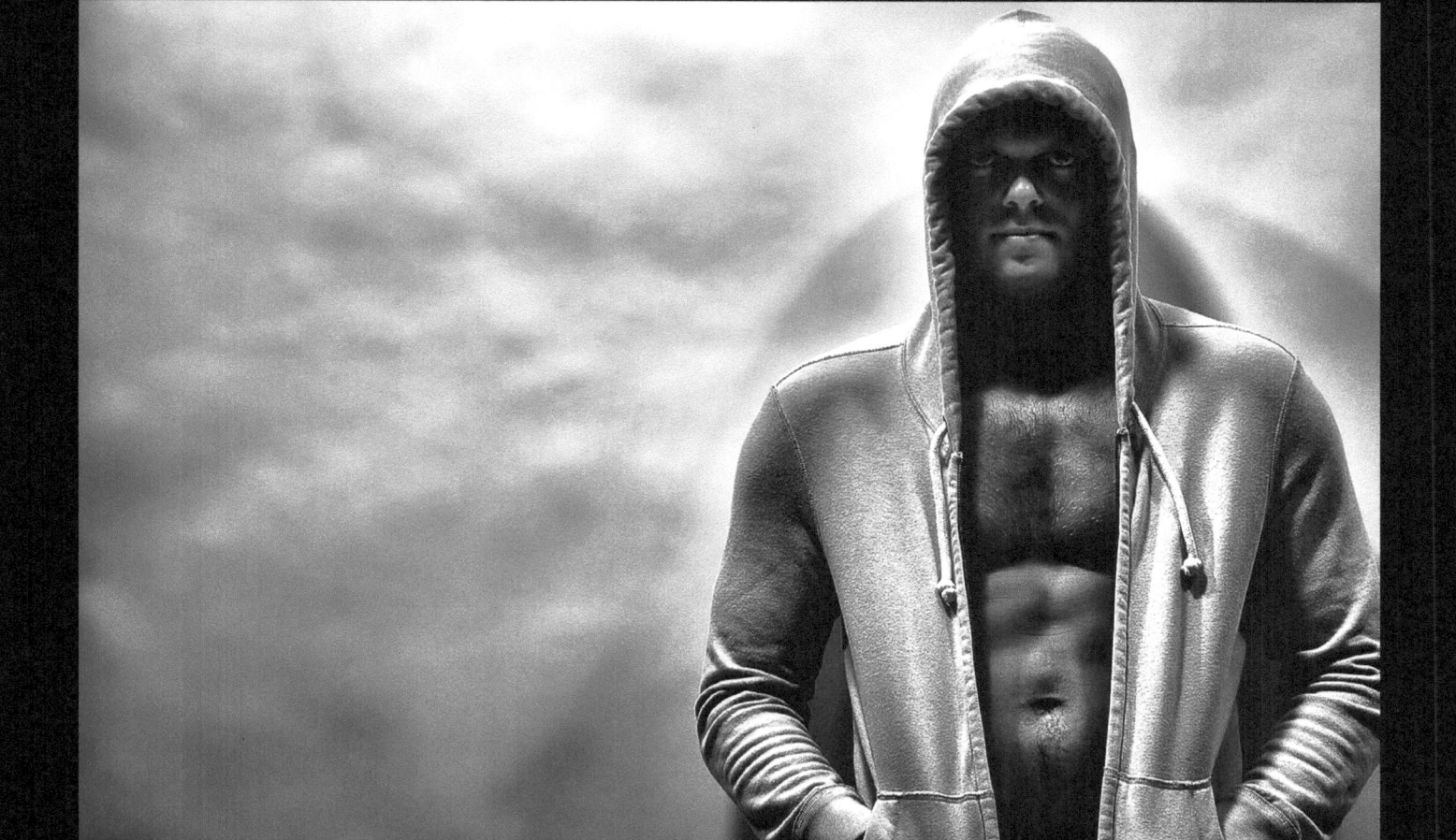

Sh wn

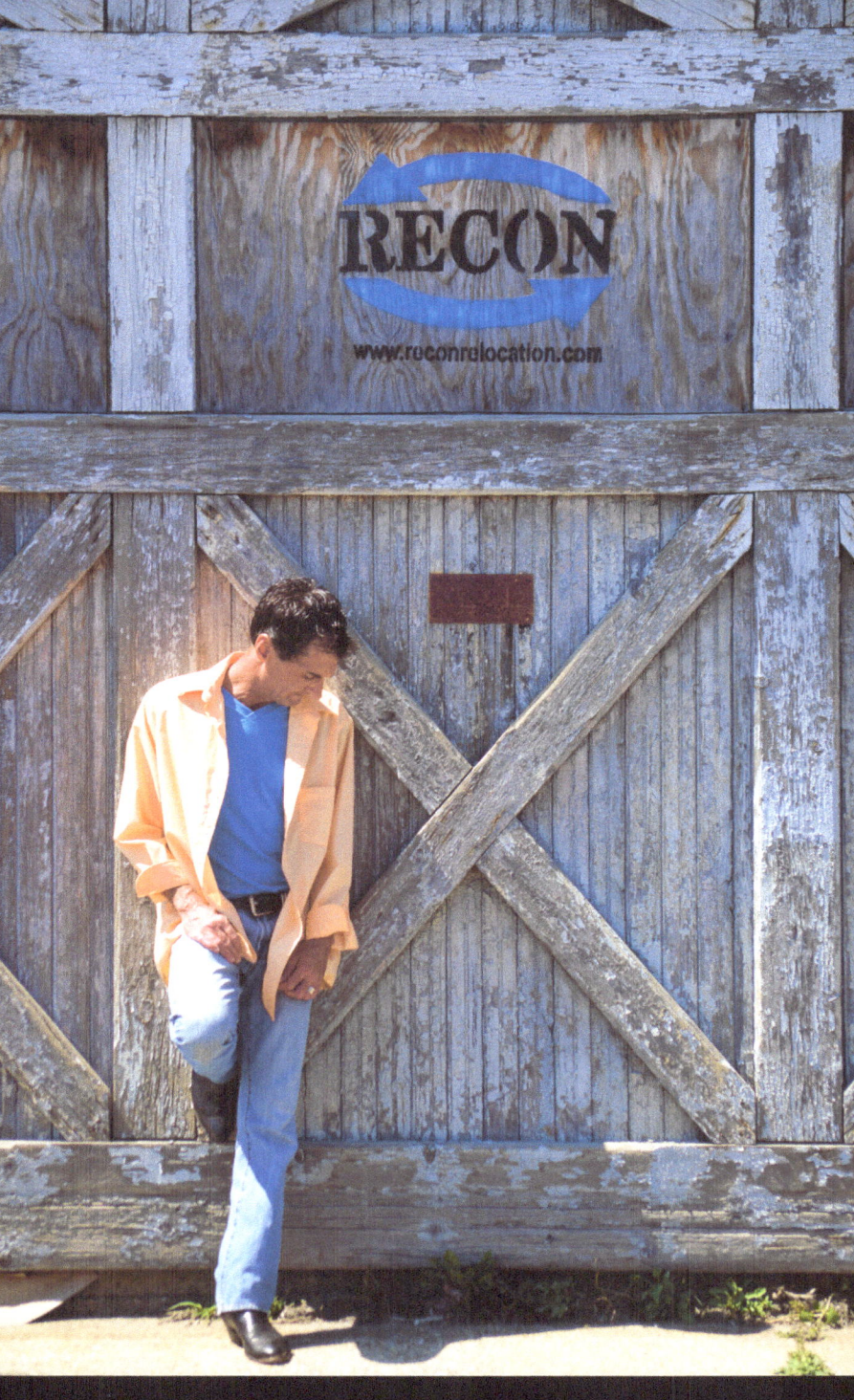

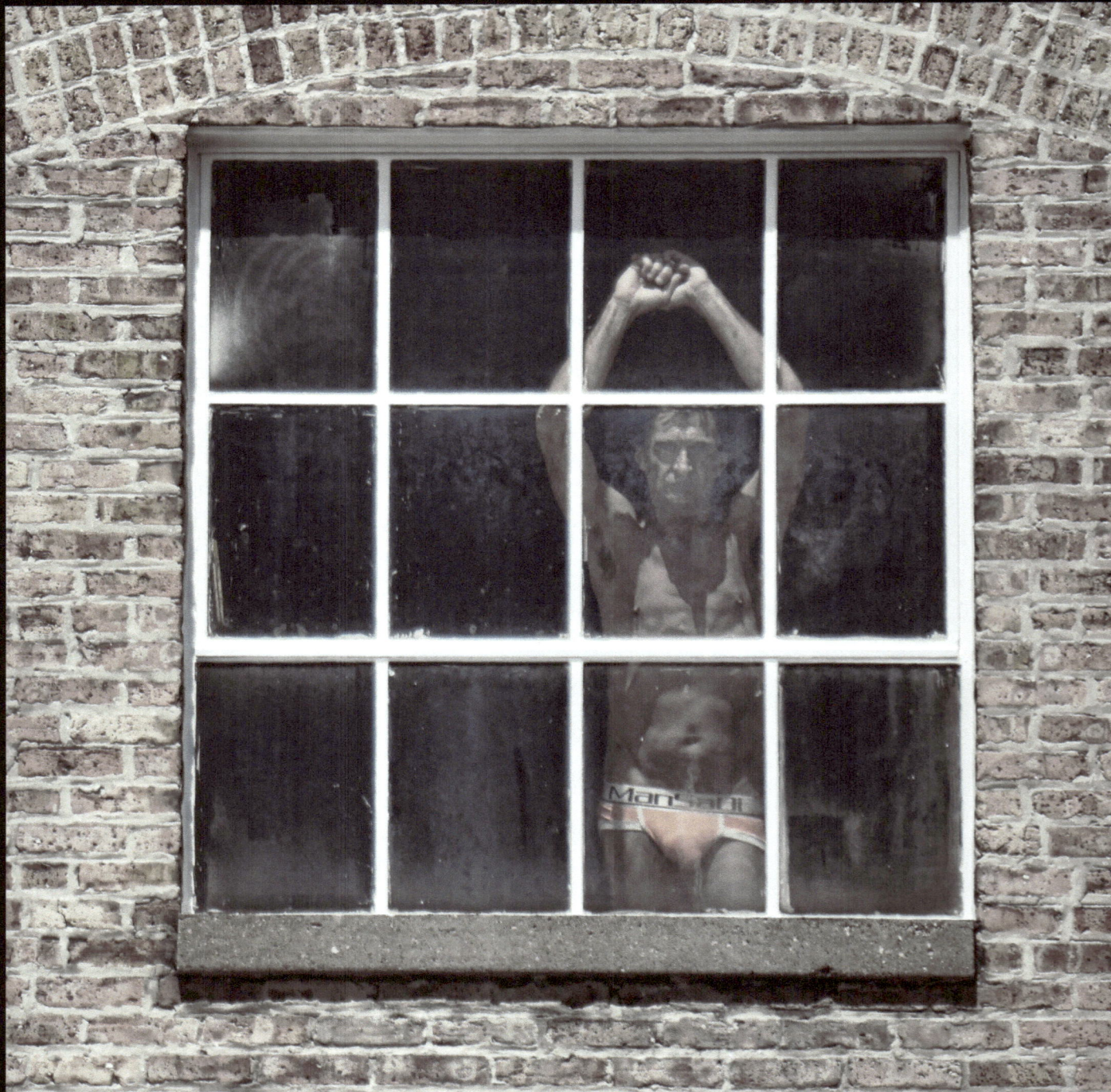

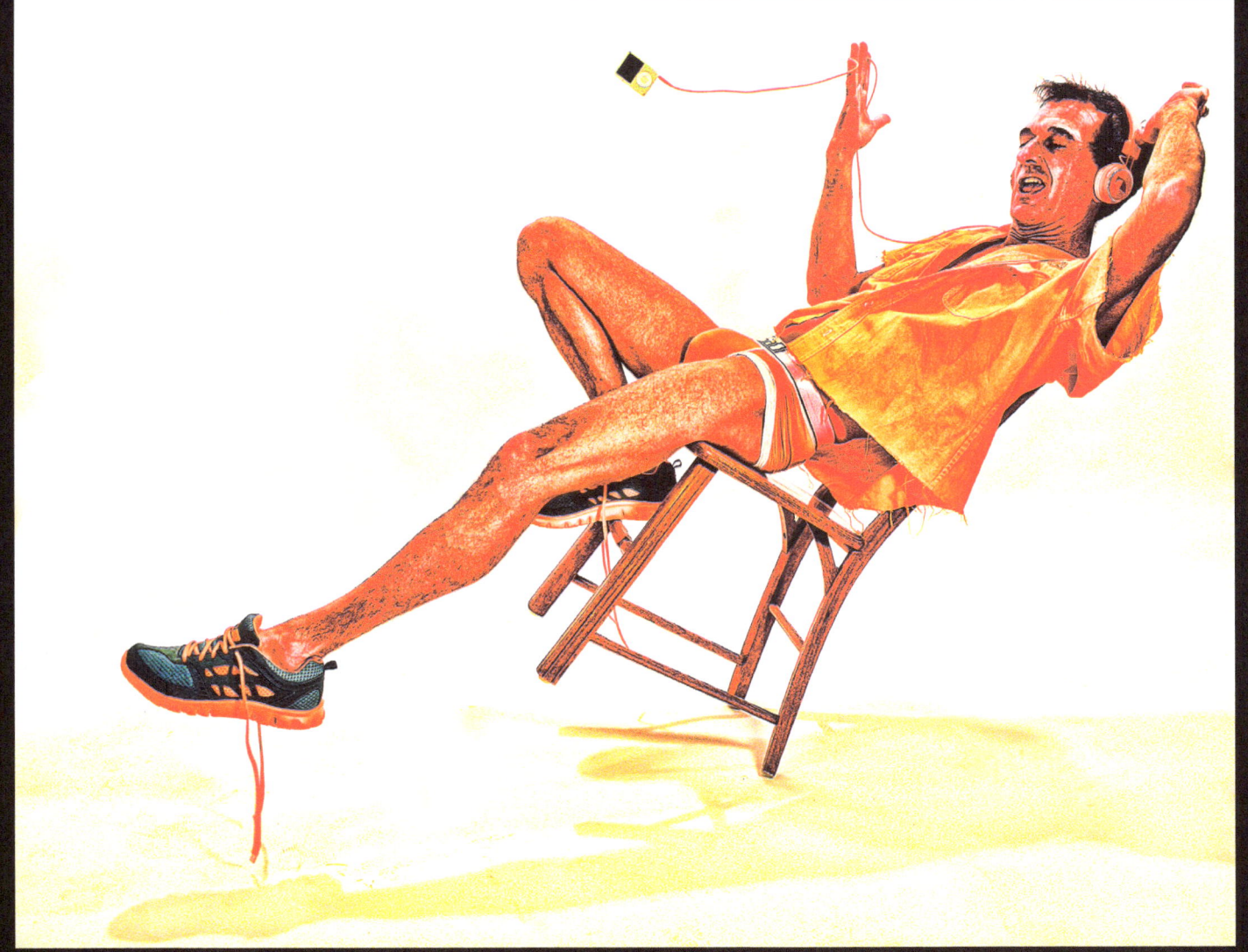

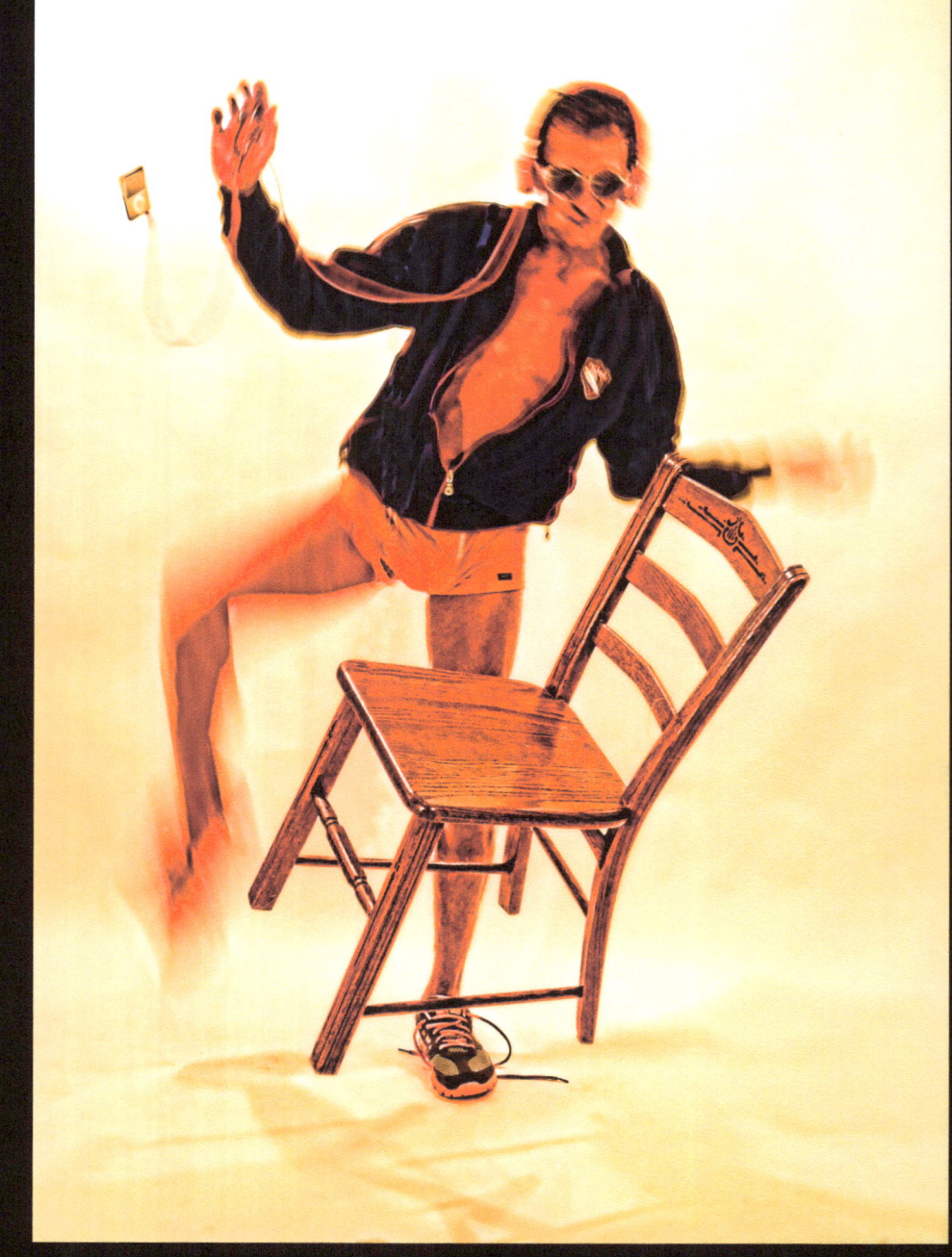

Prince

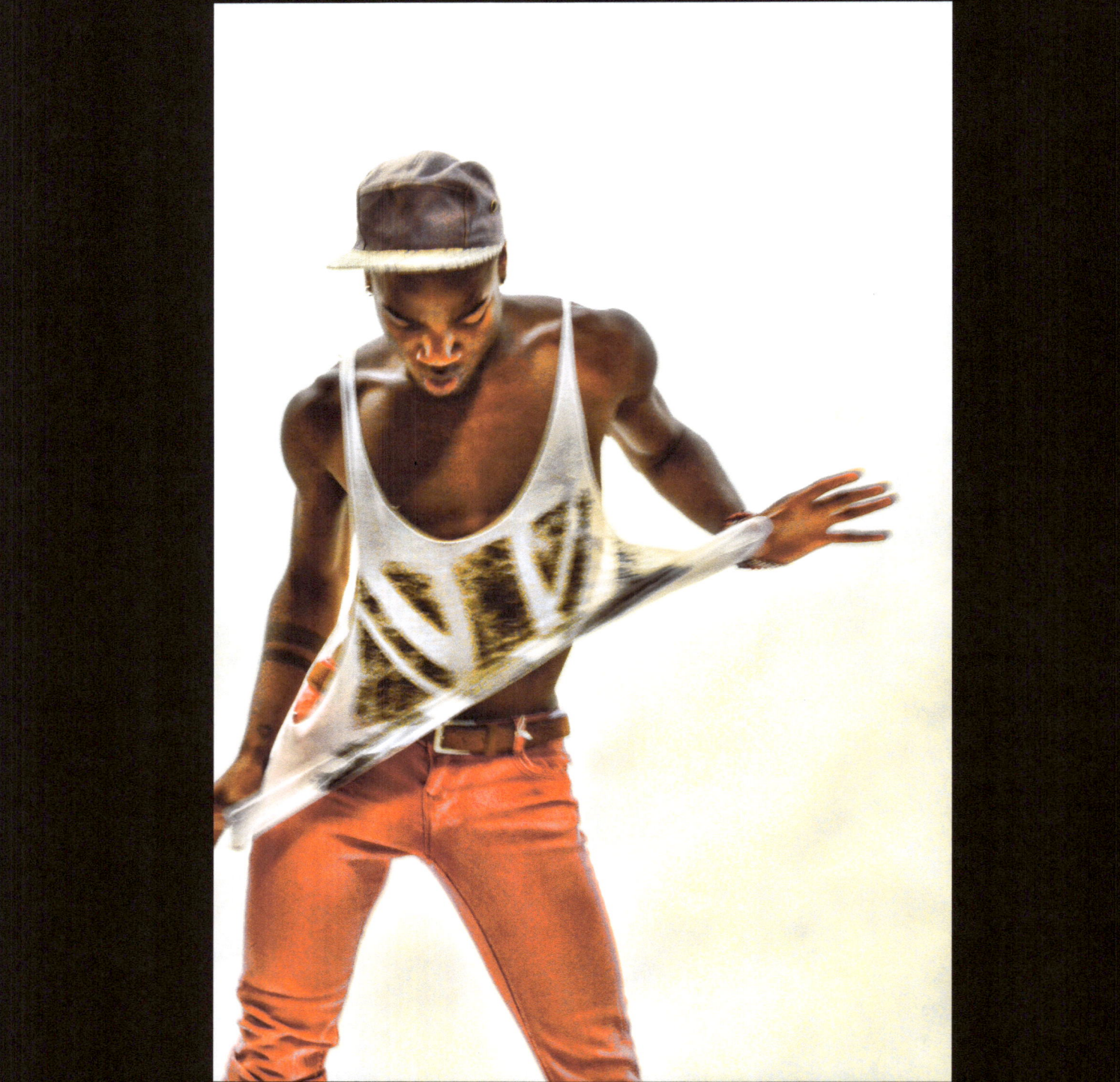

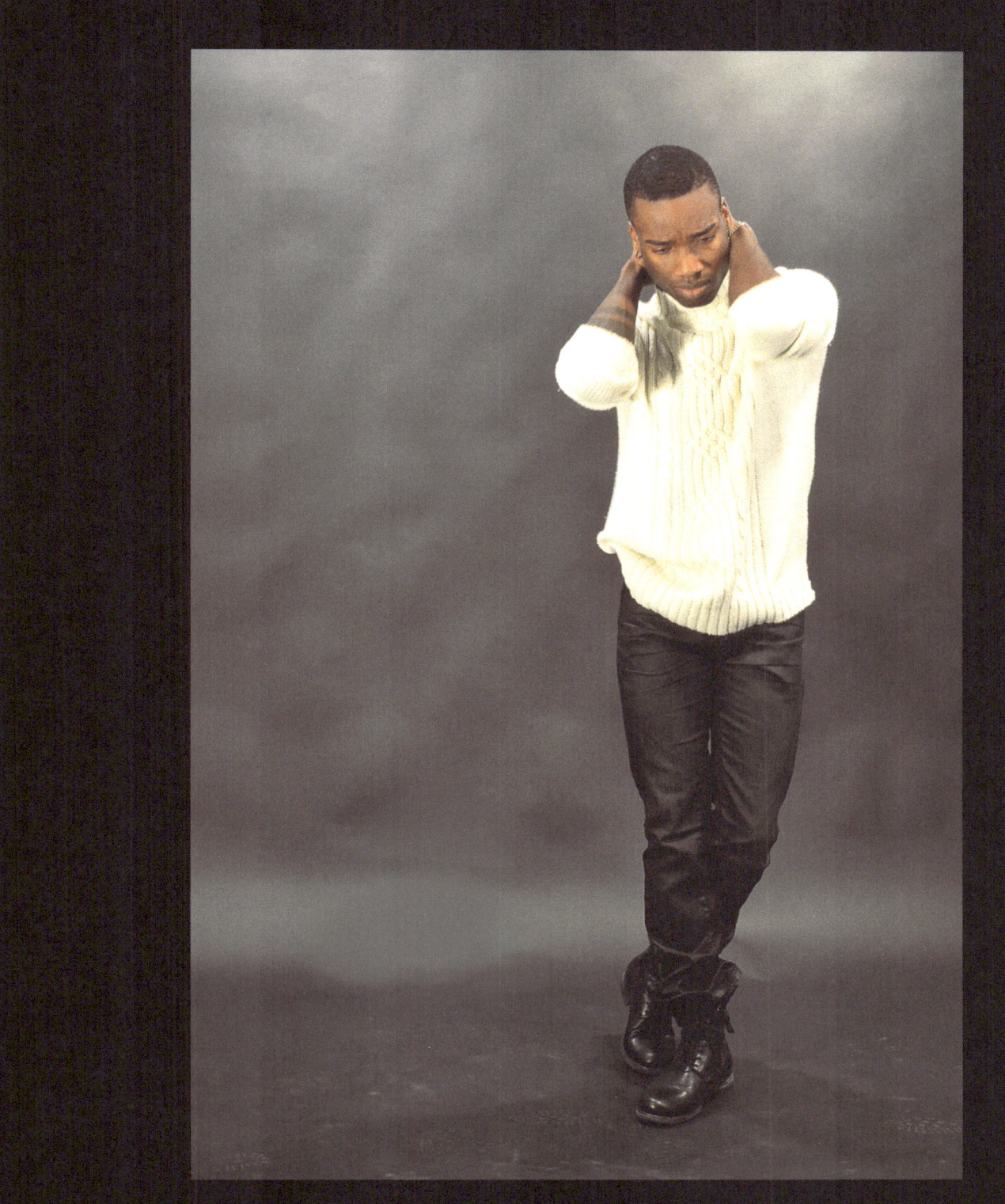

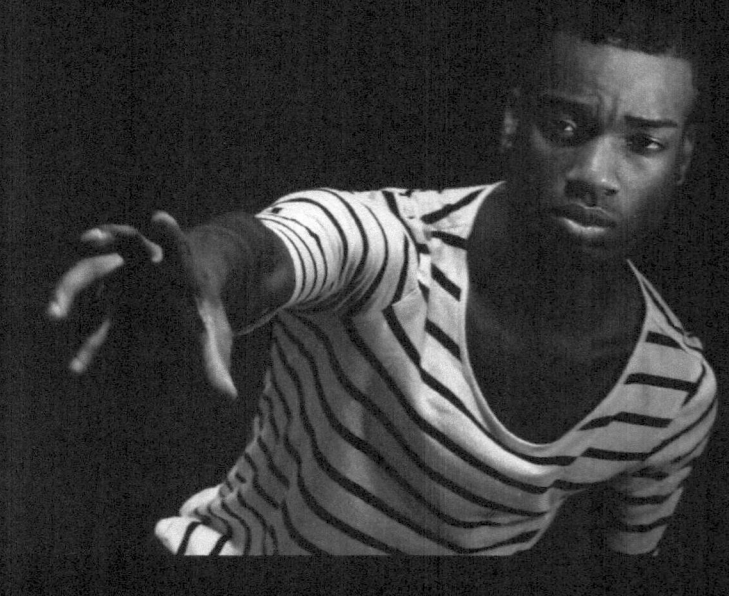

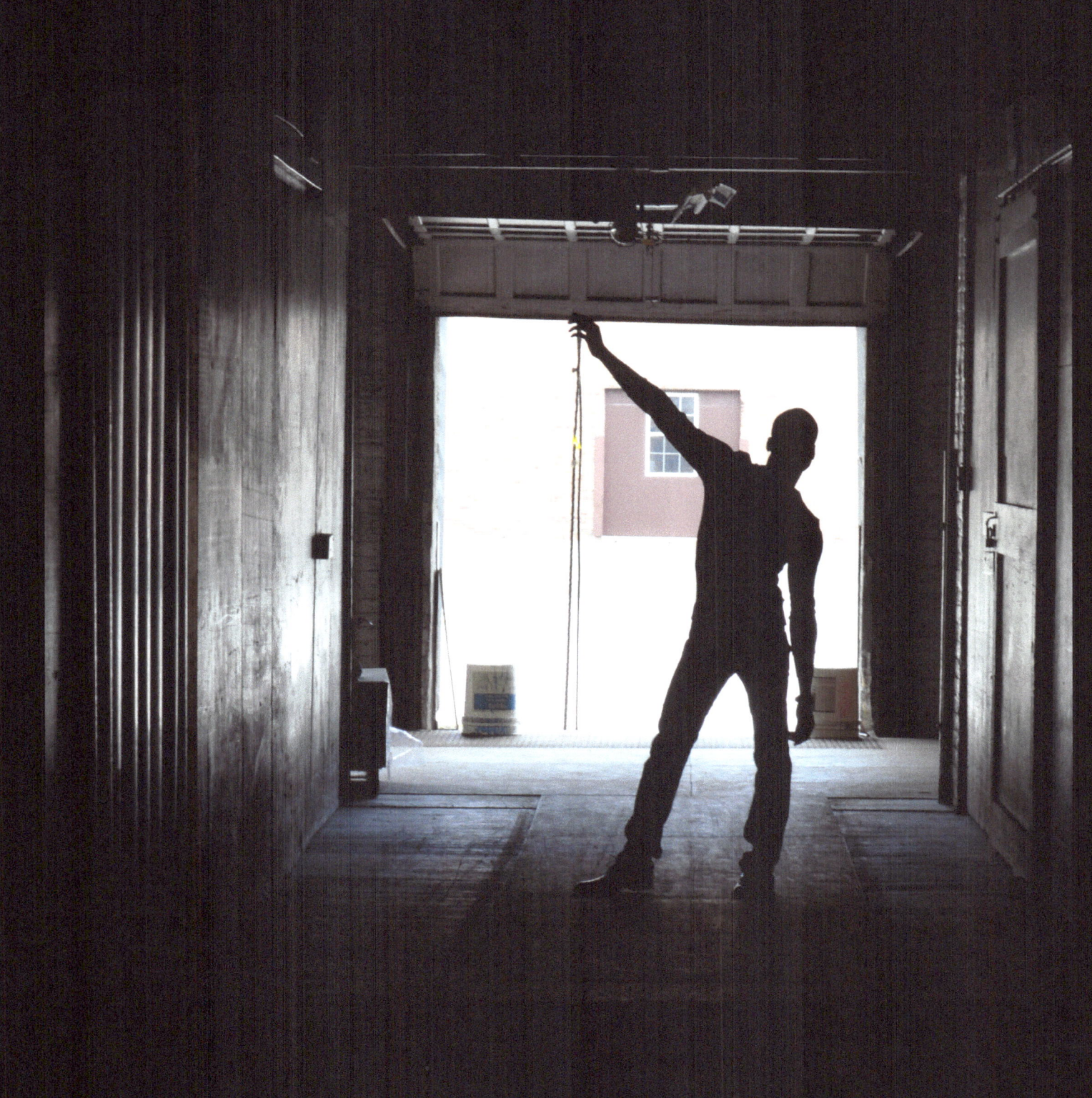

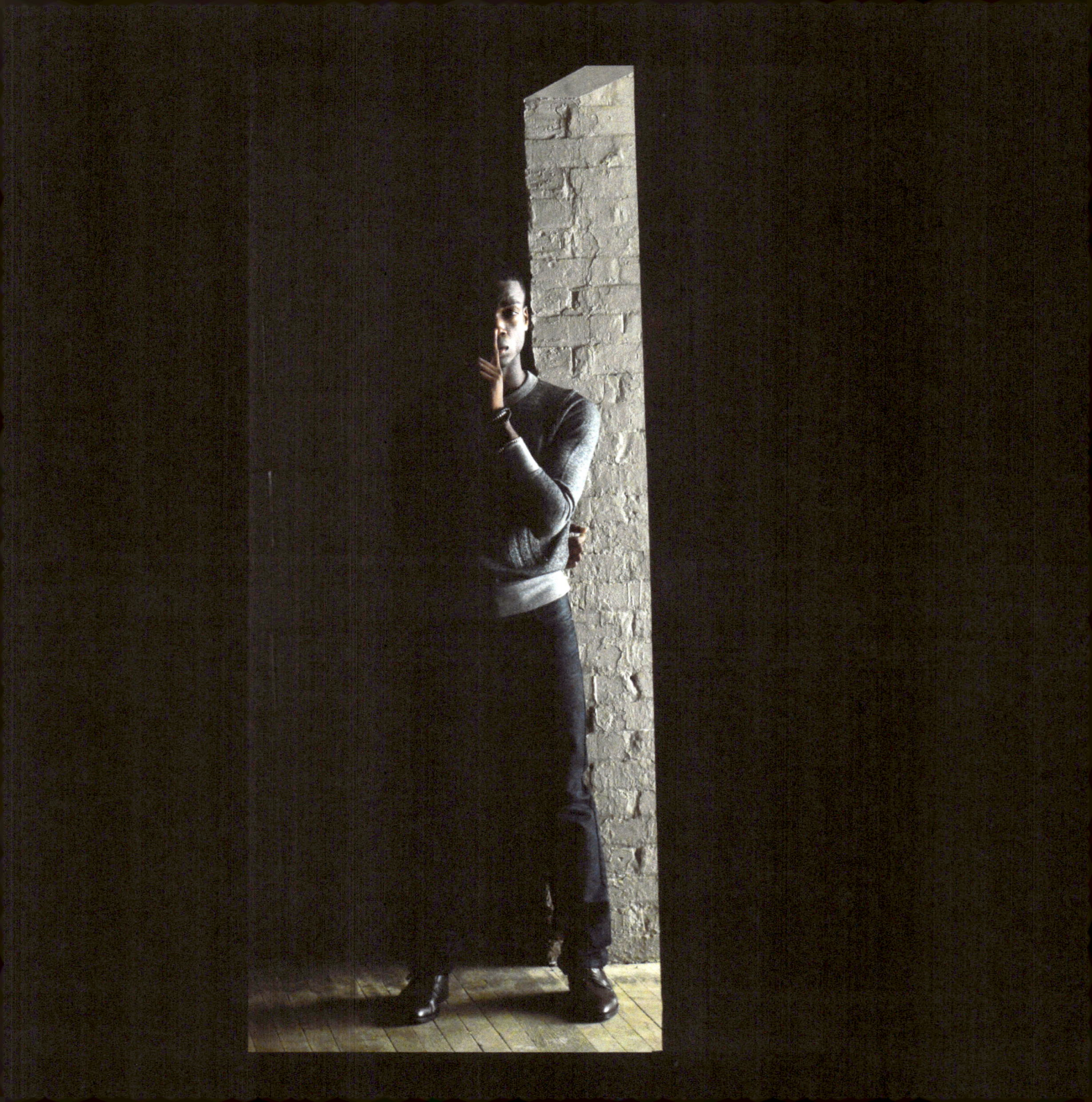

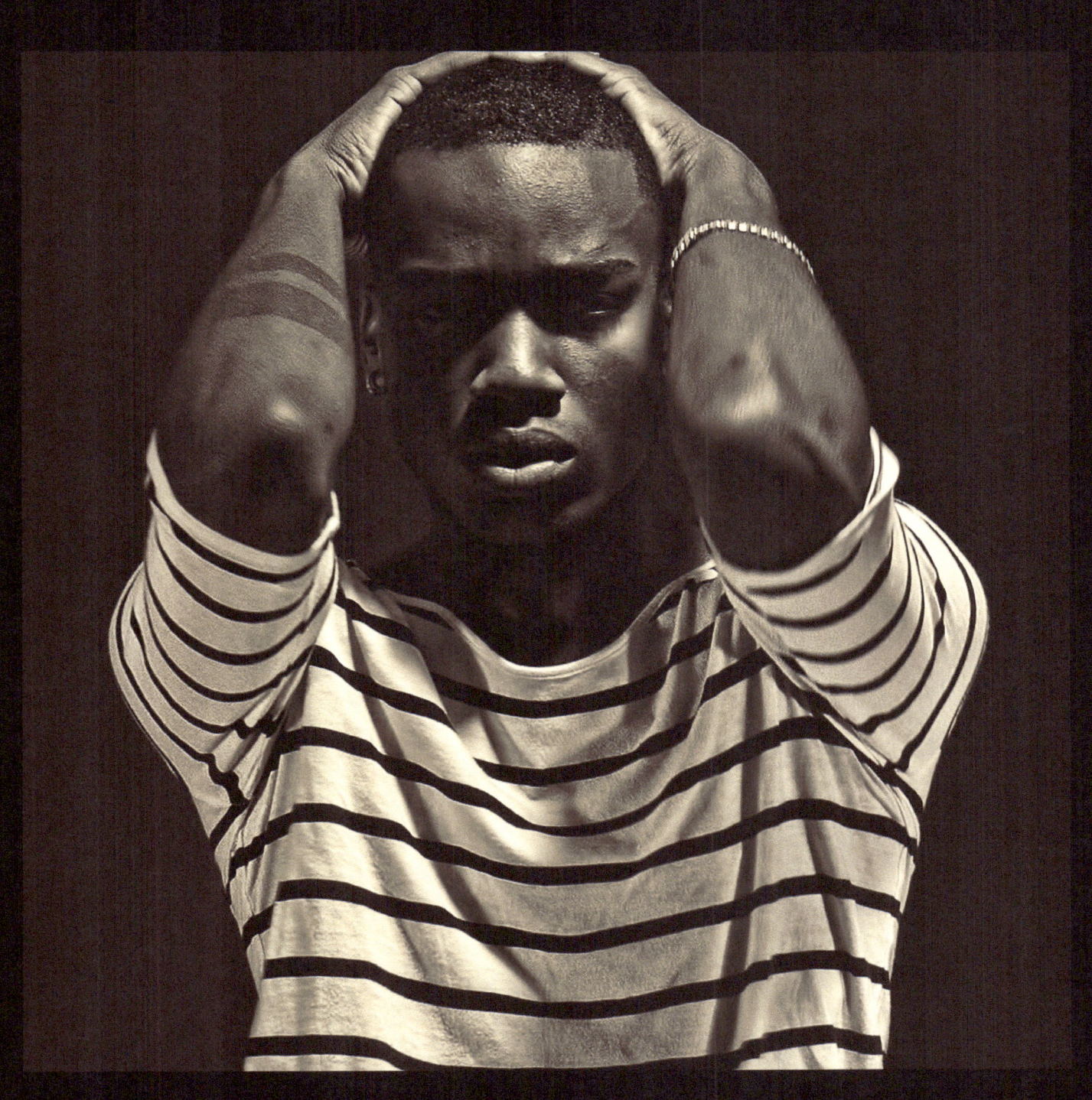

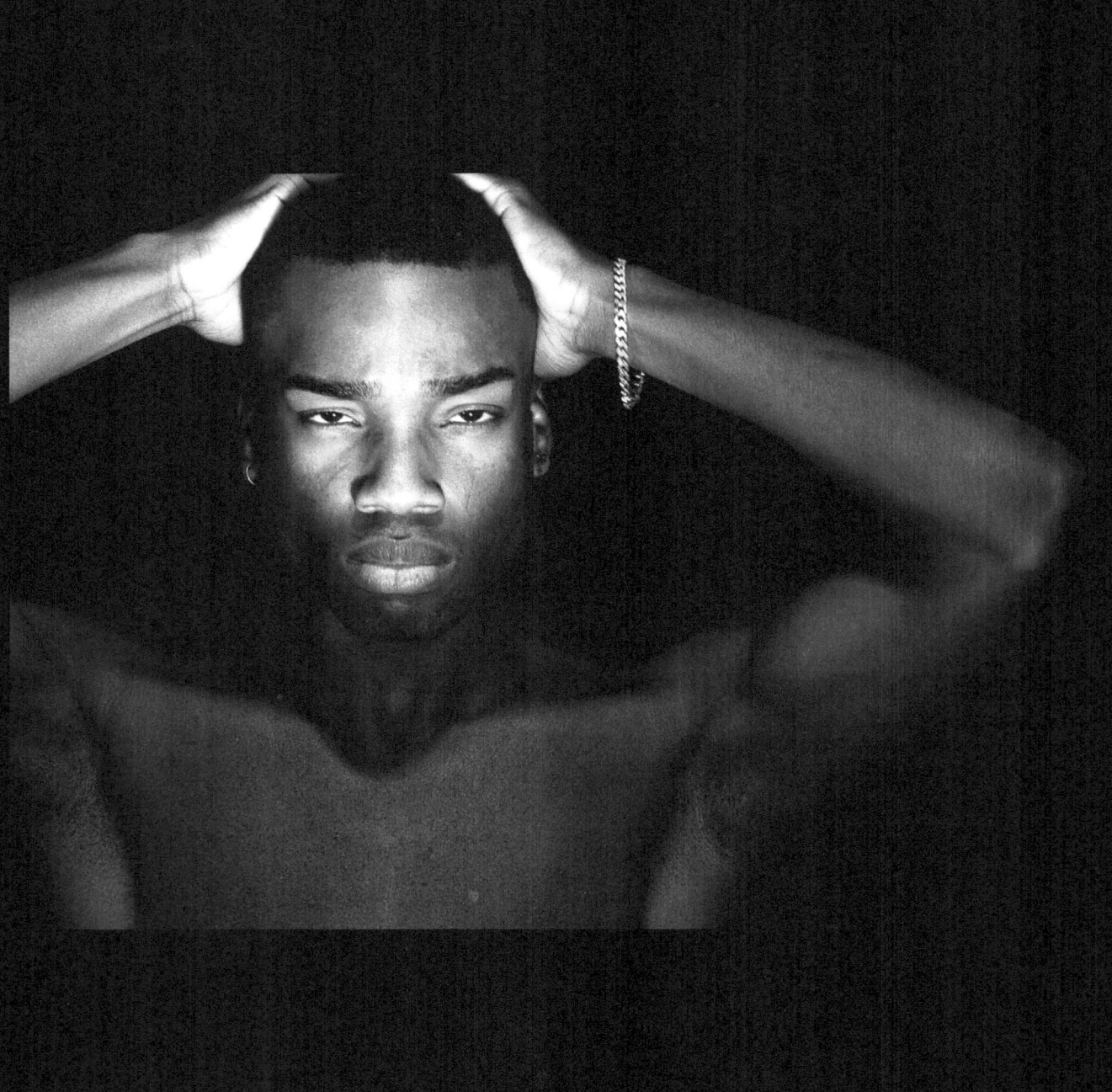

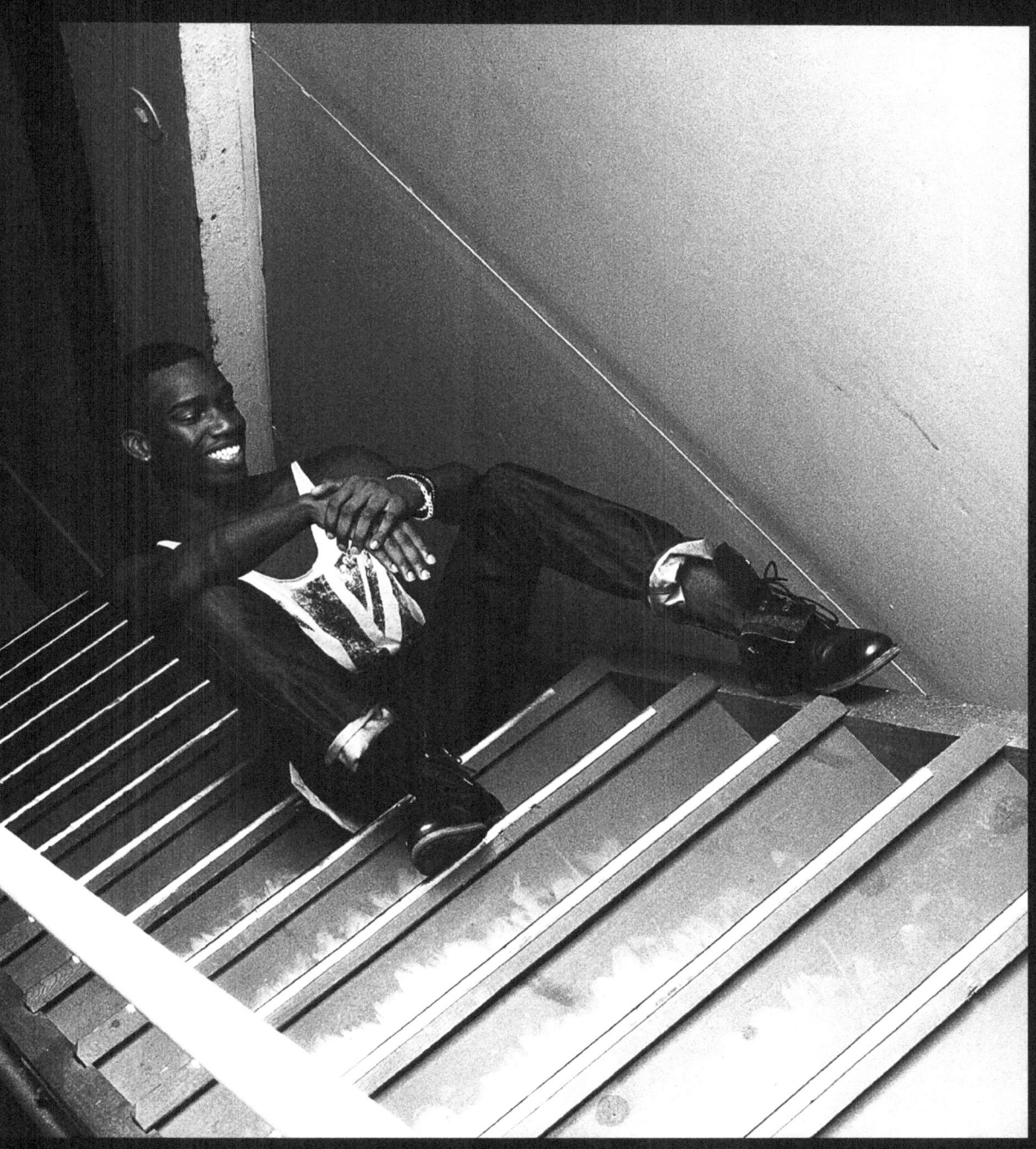

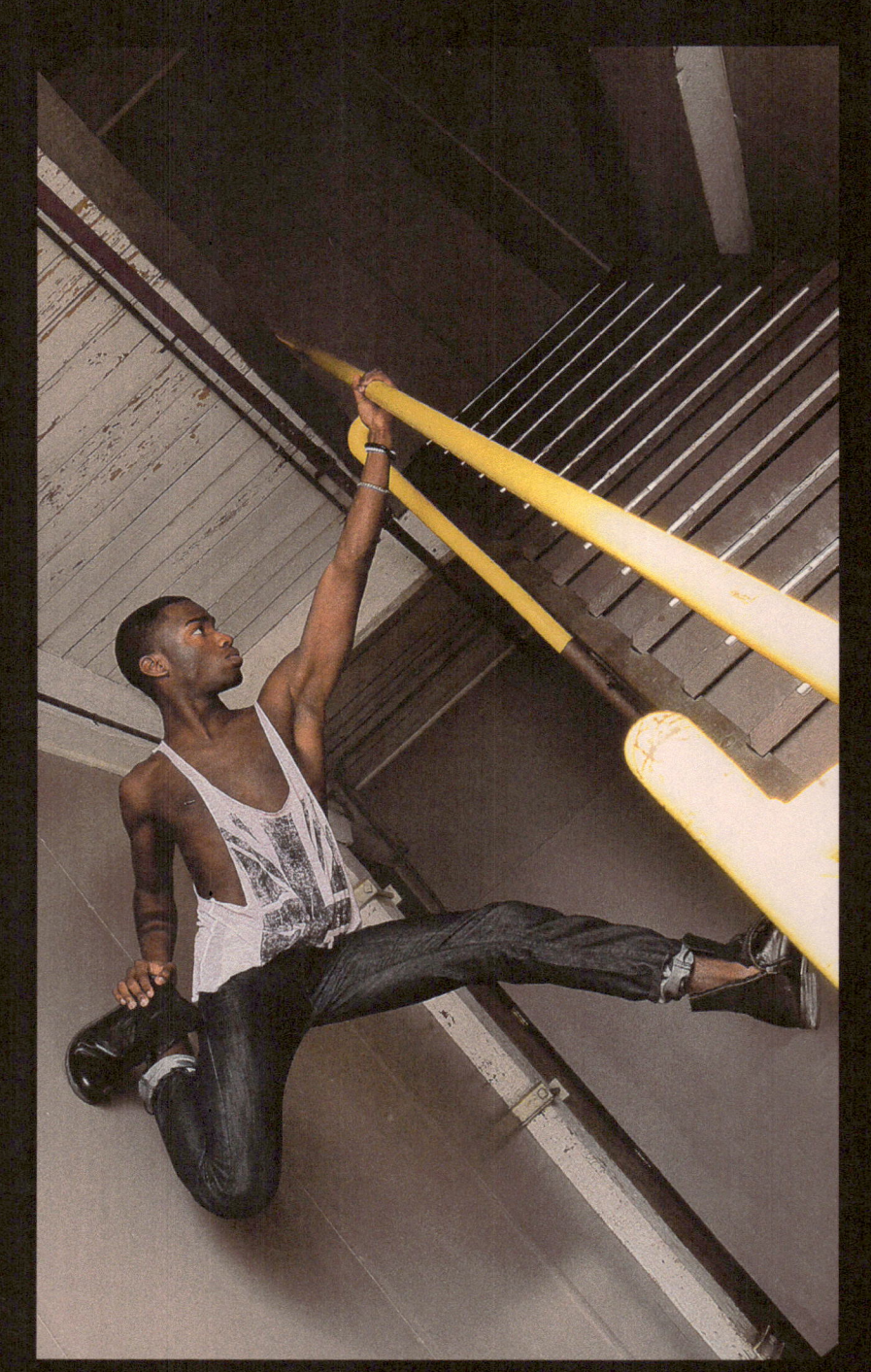

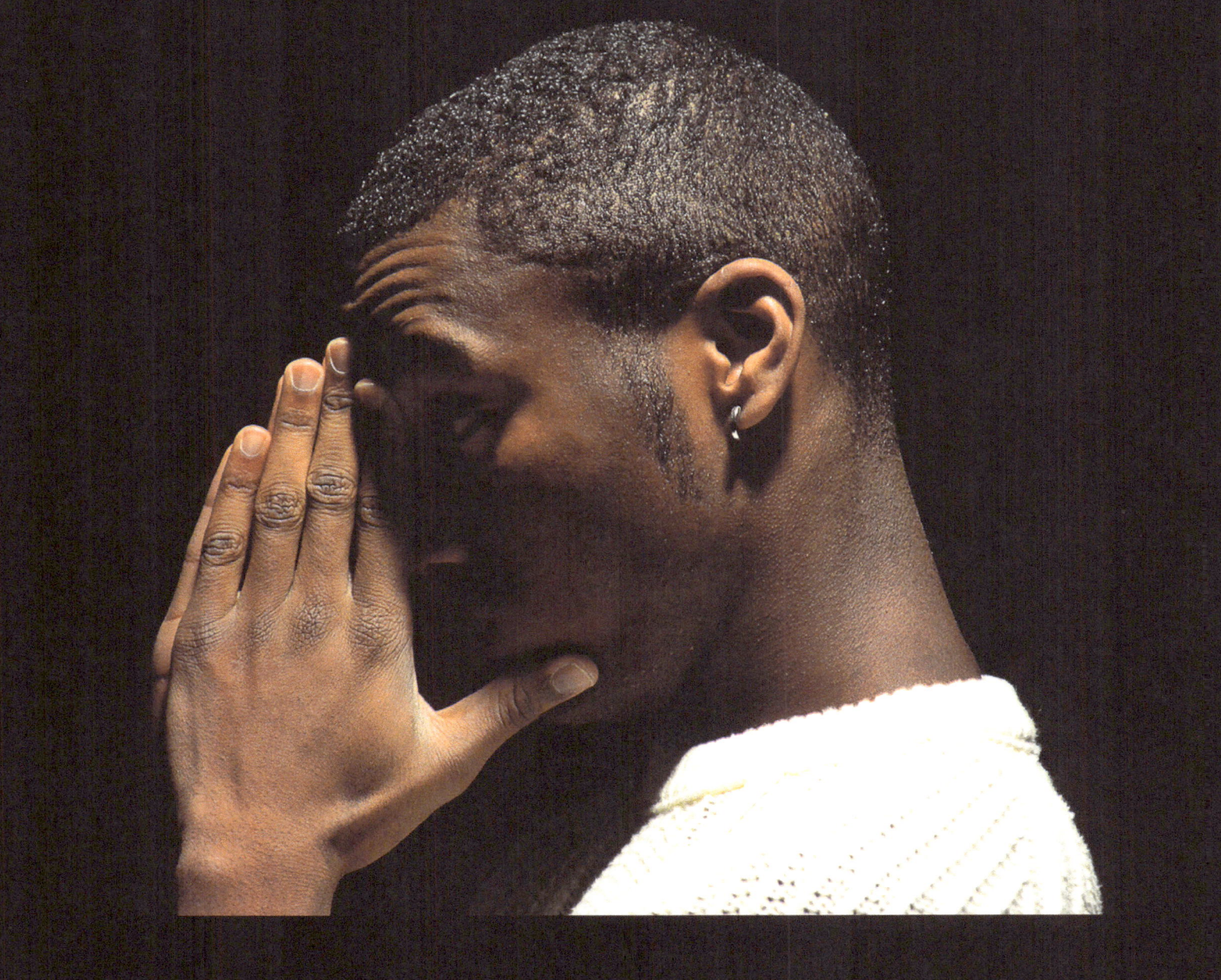

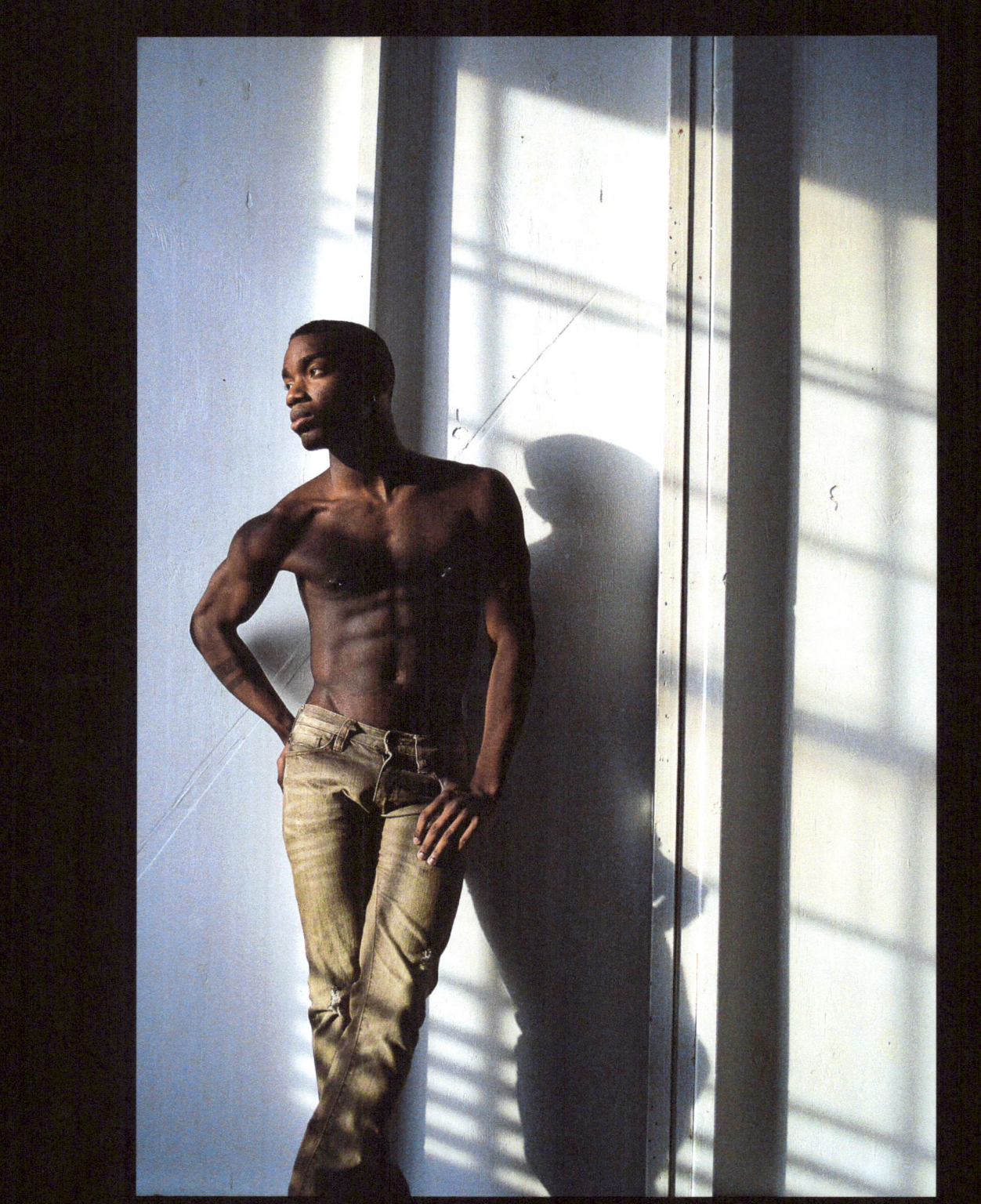

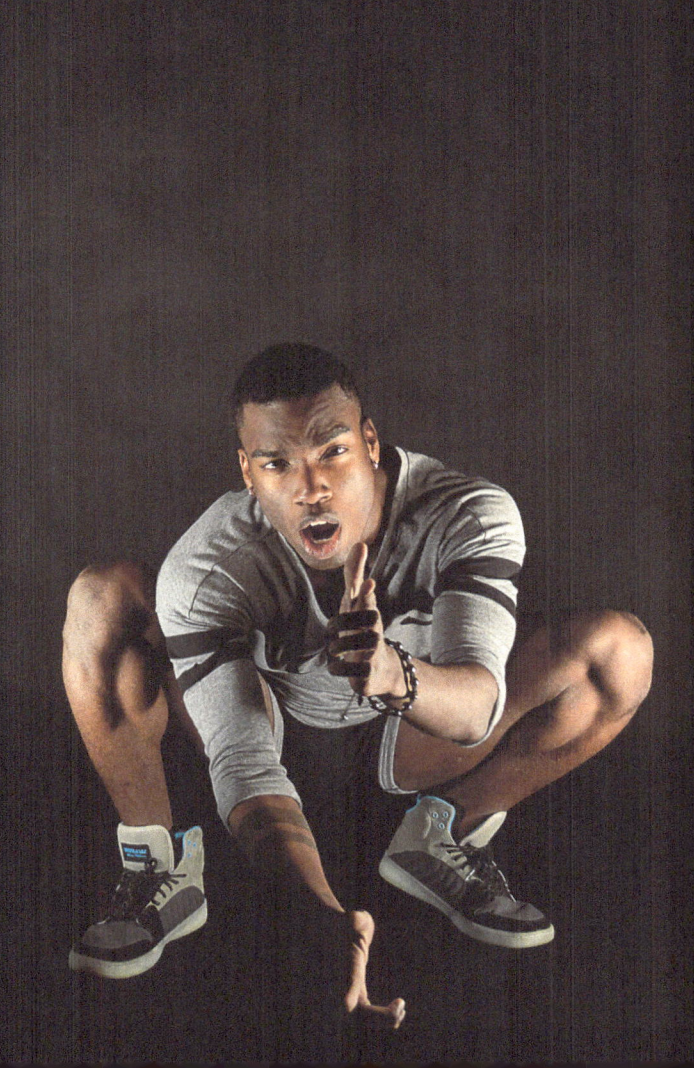

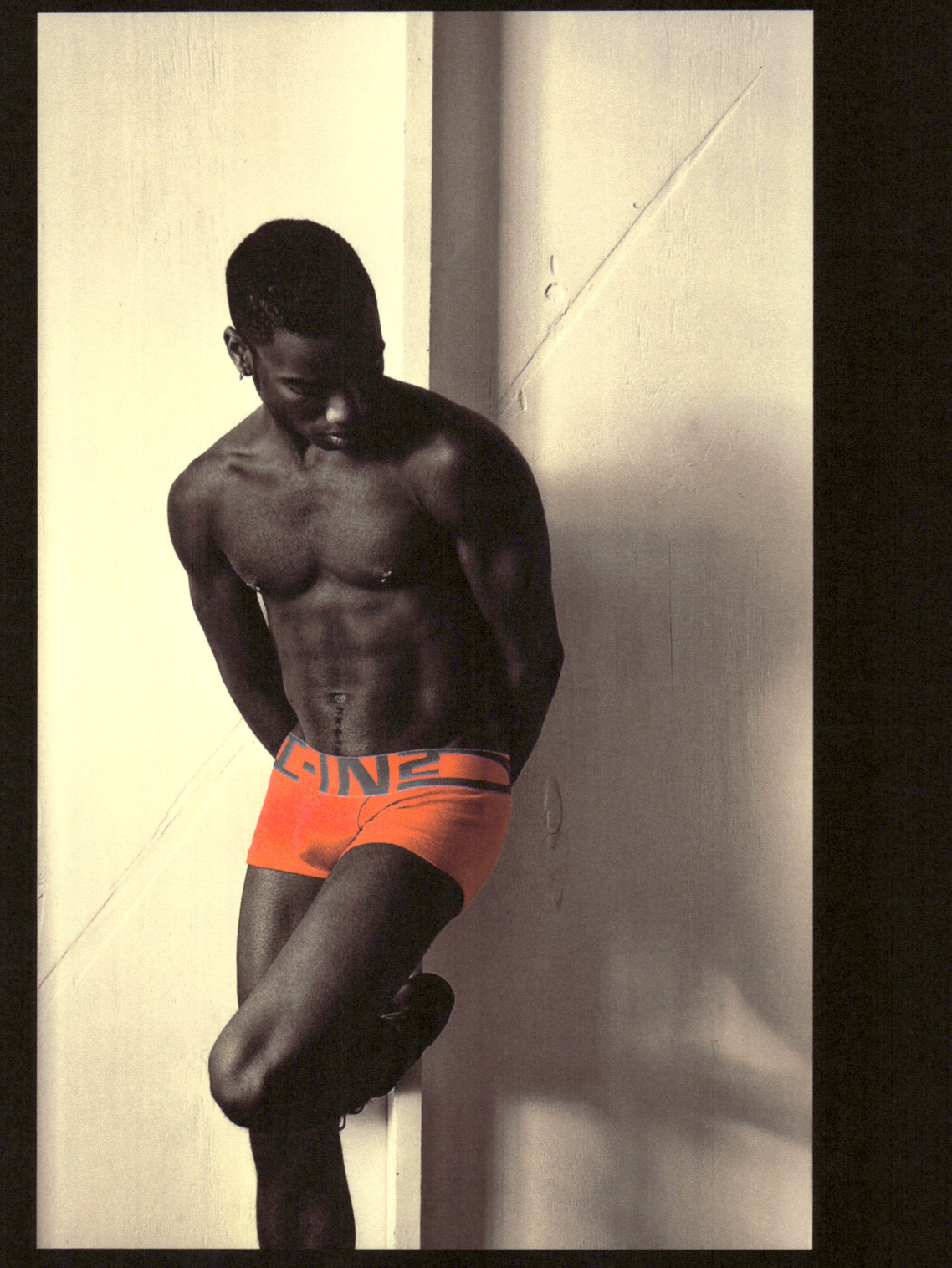

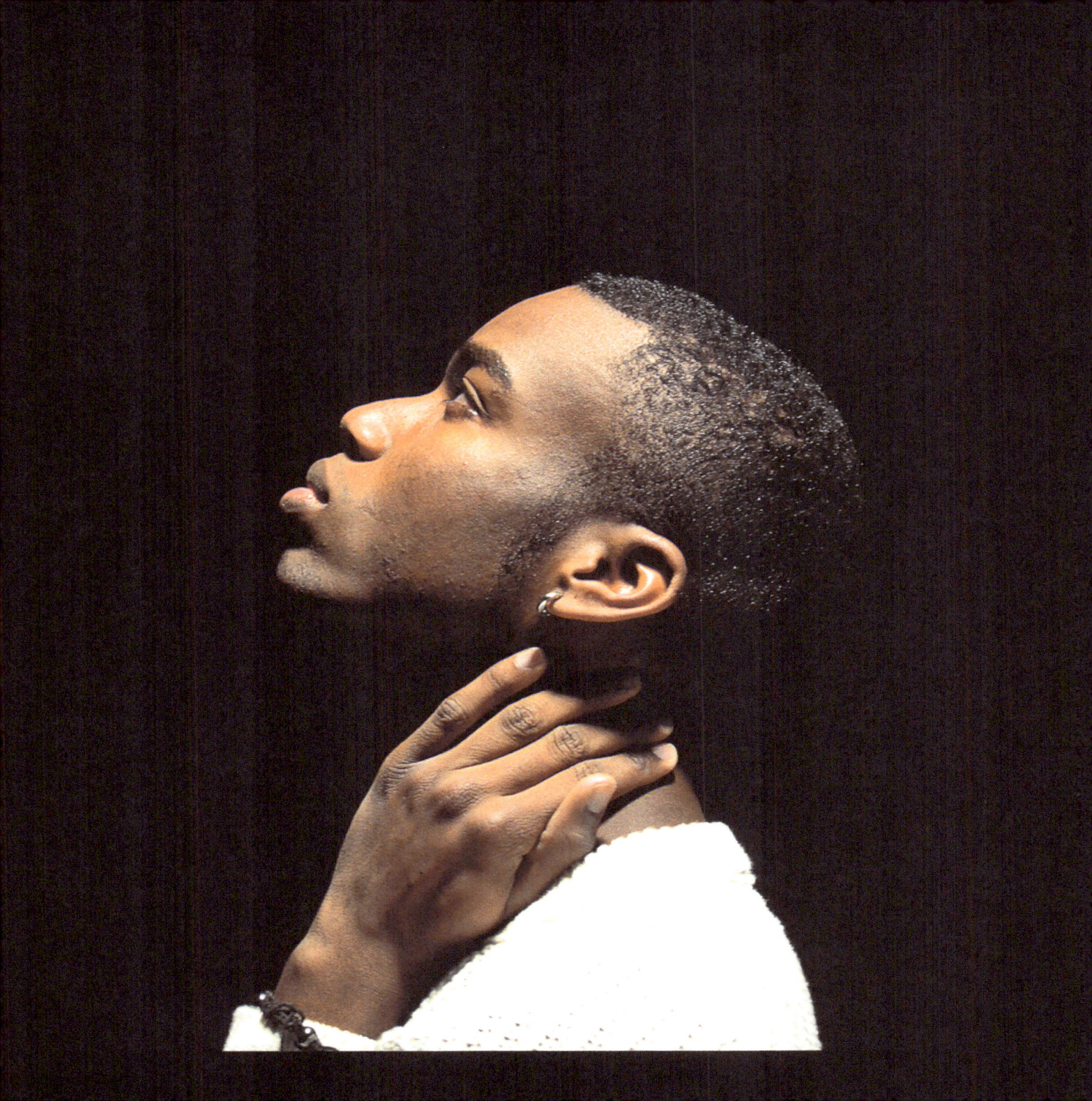

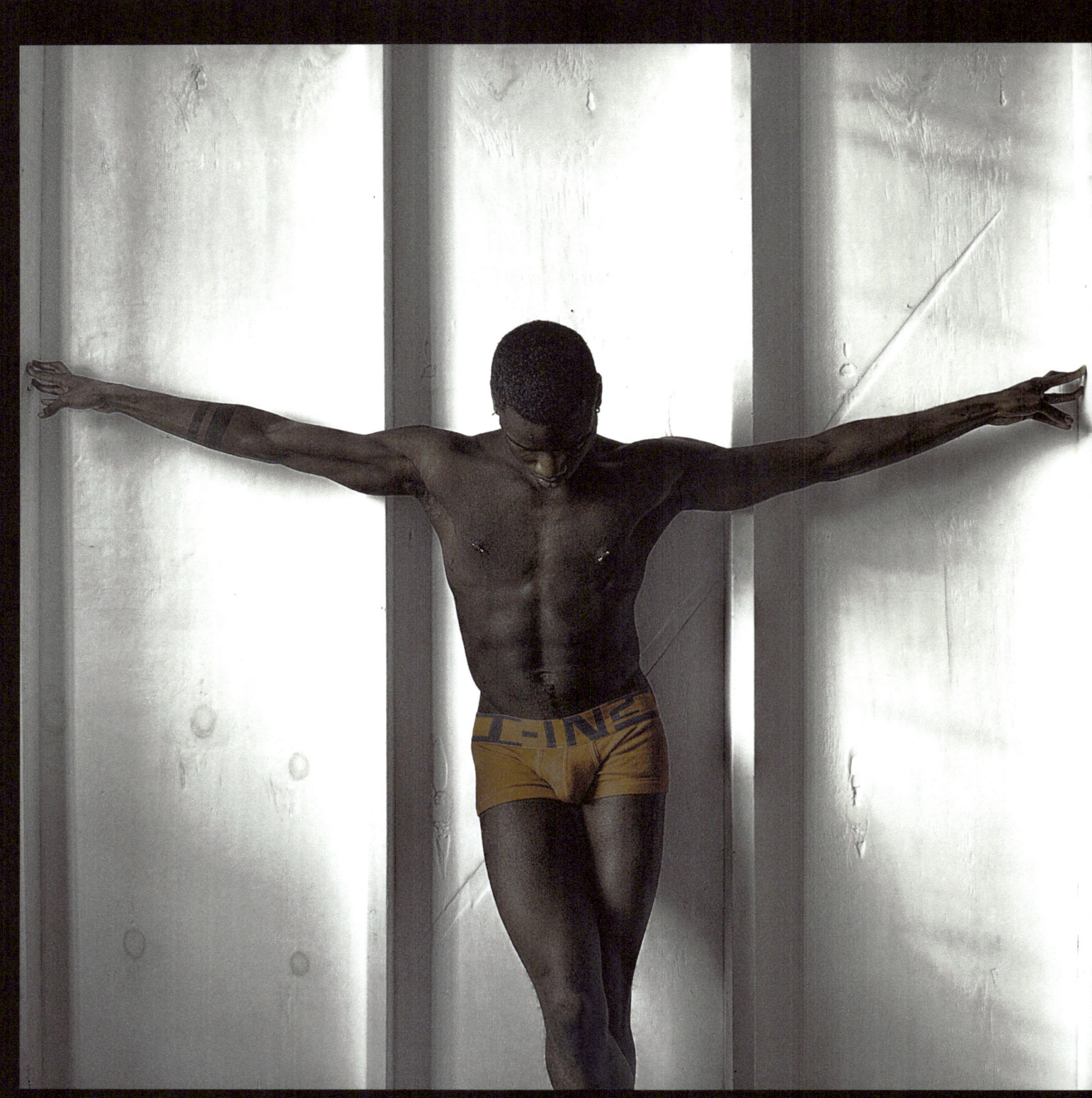

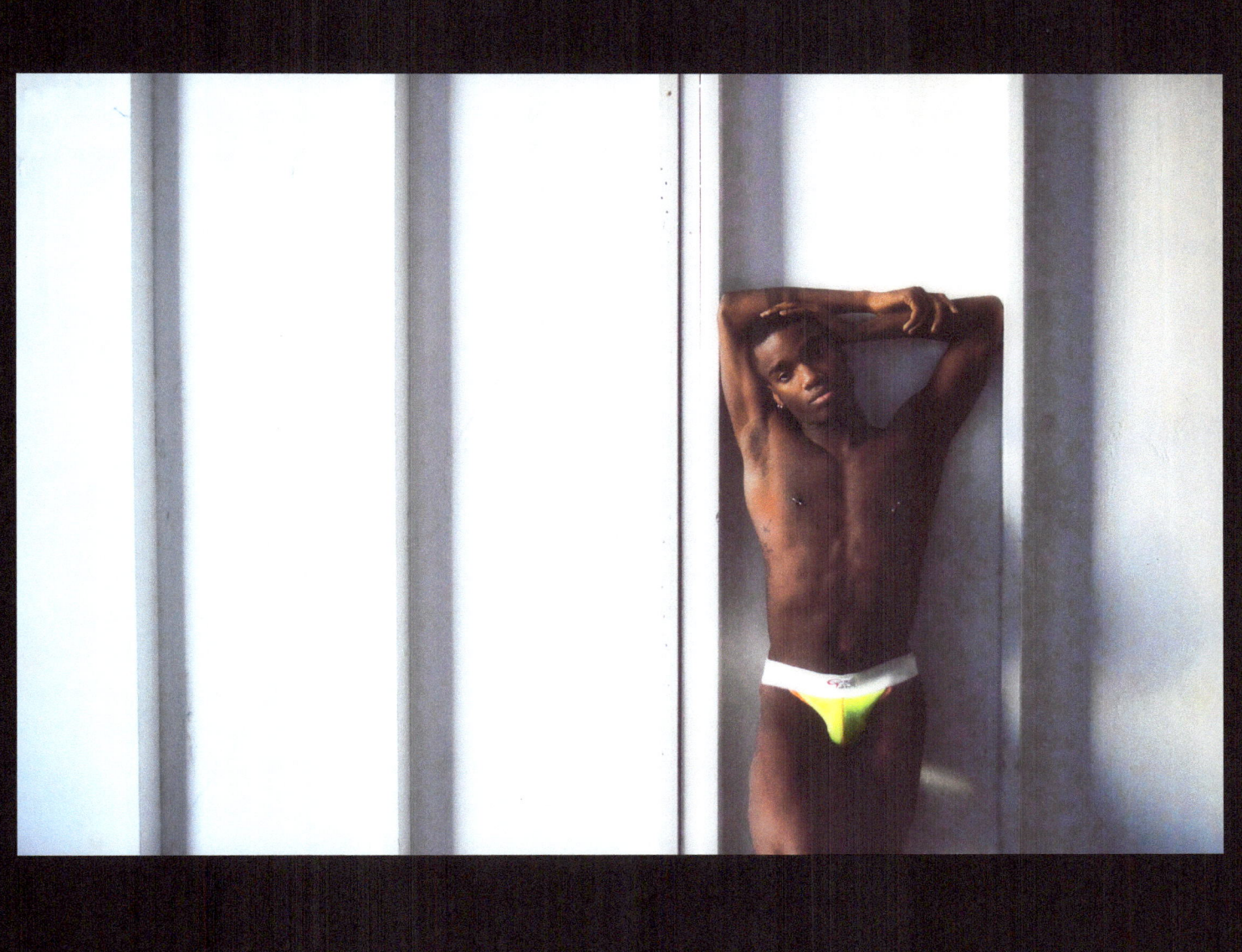

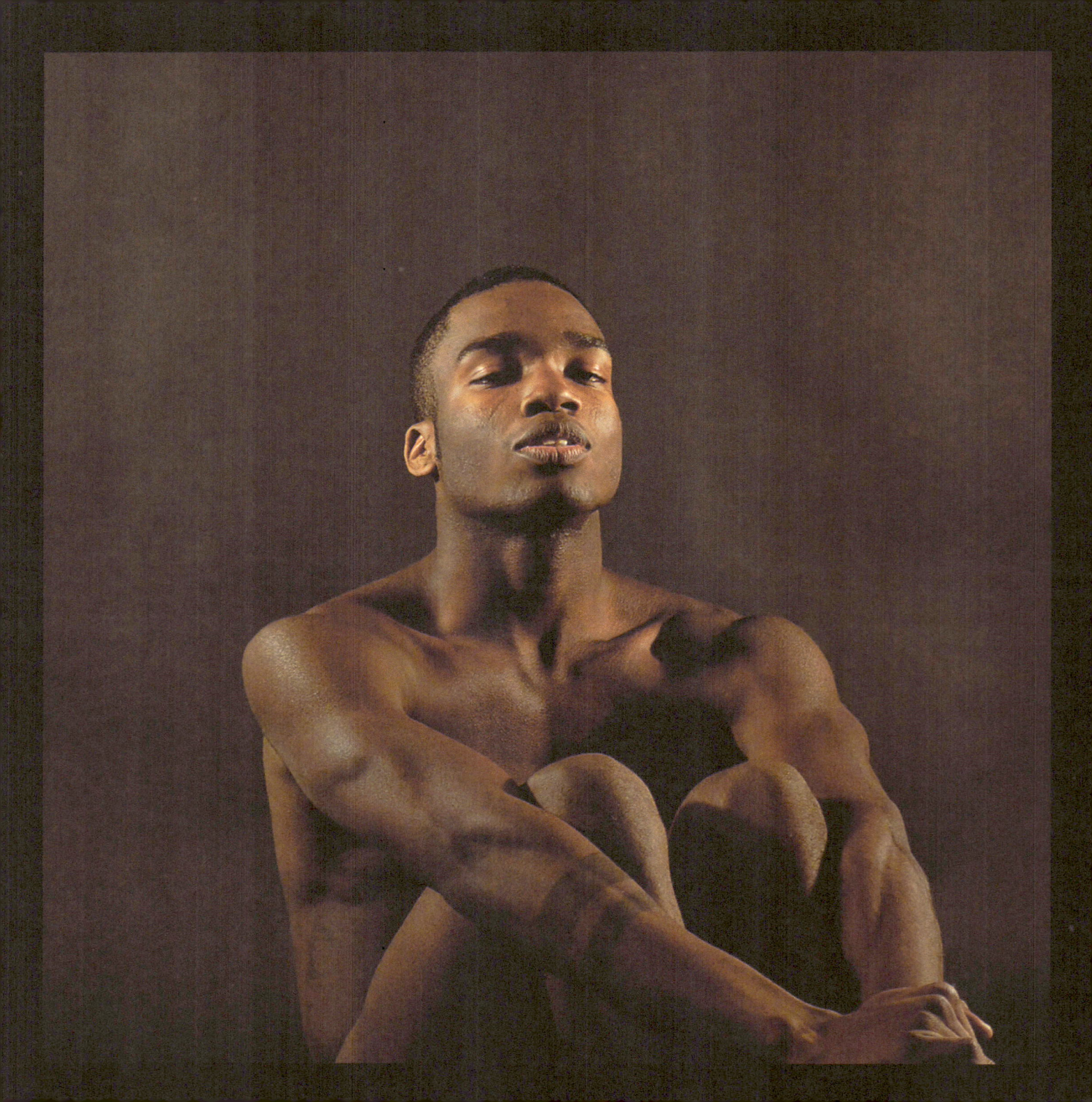

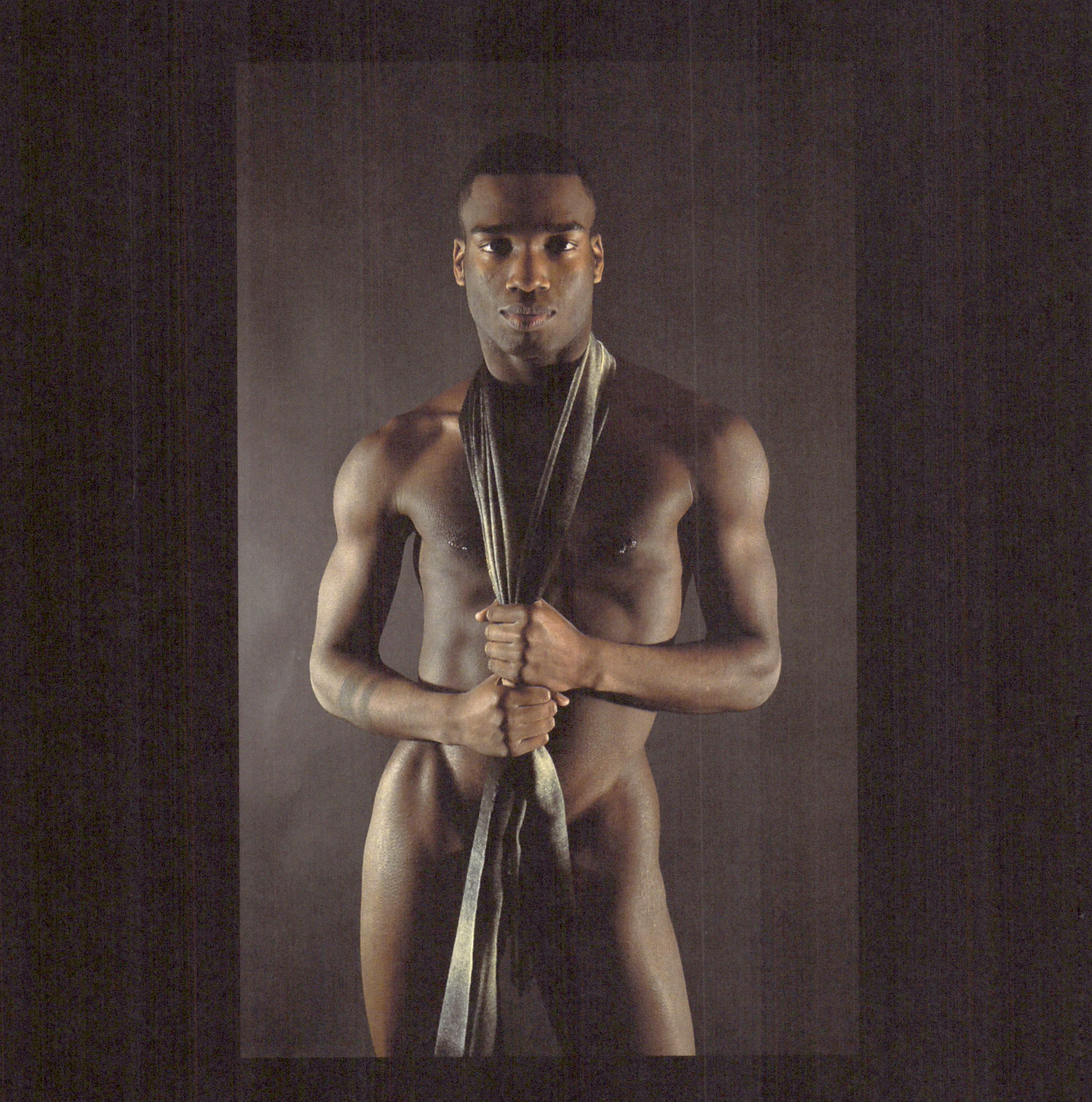

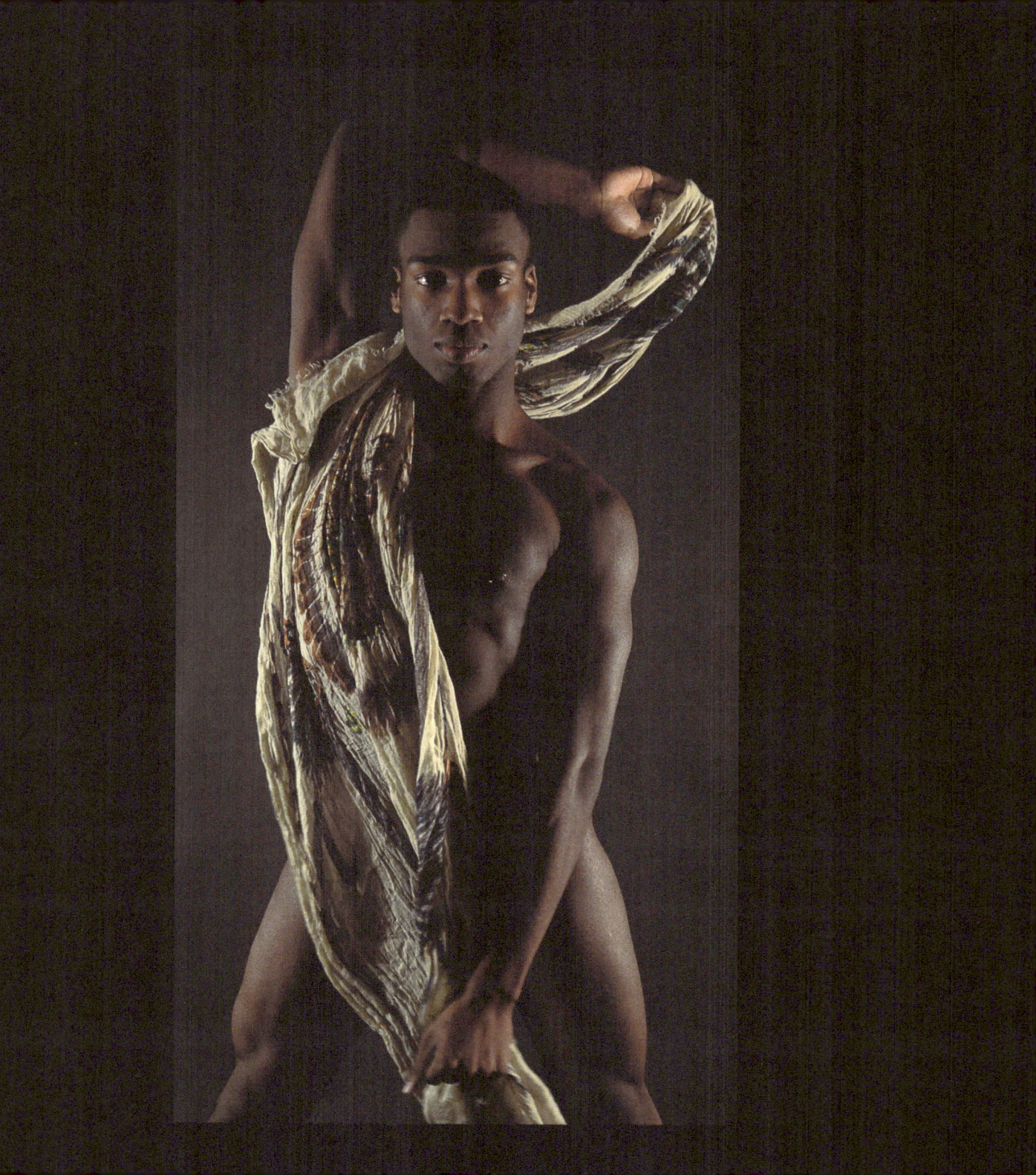

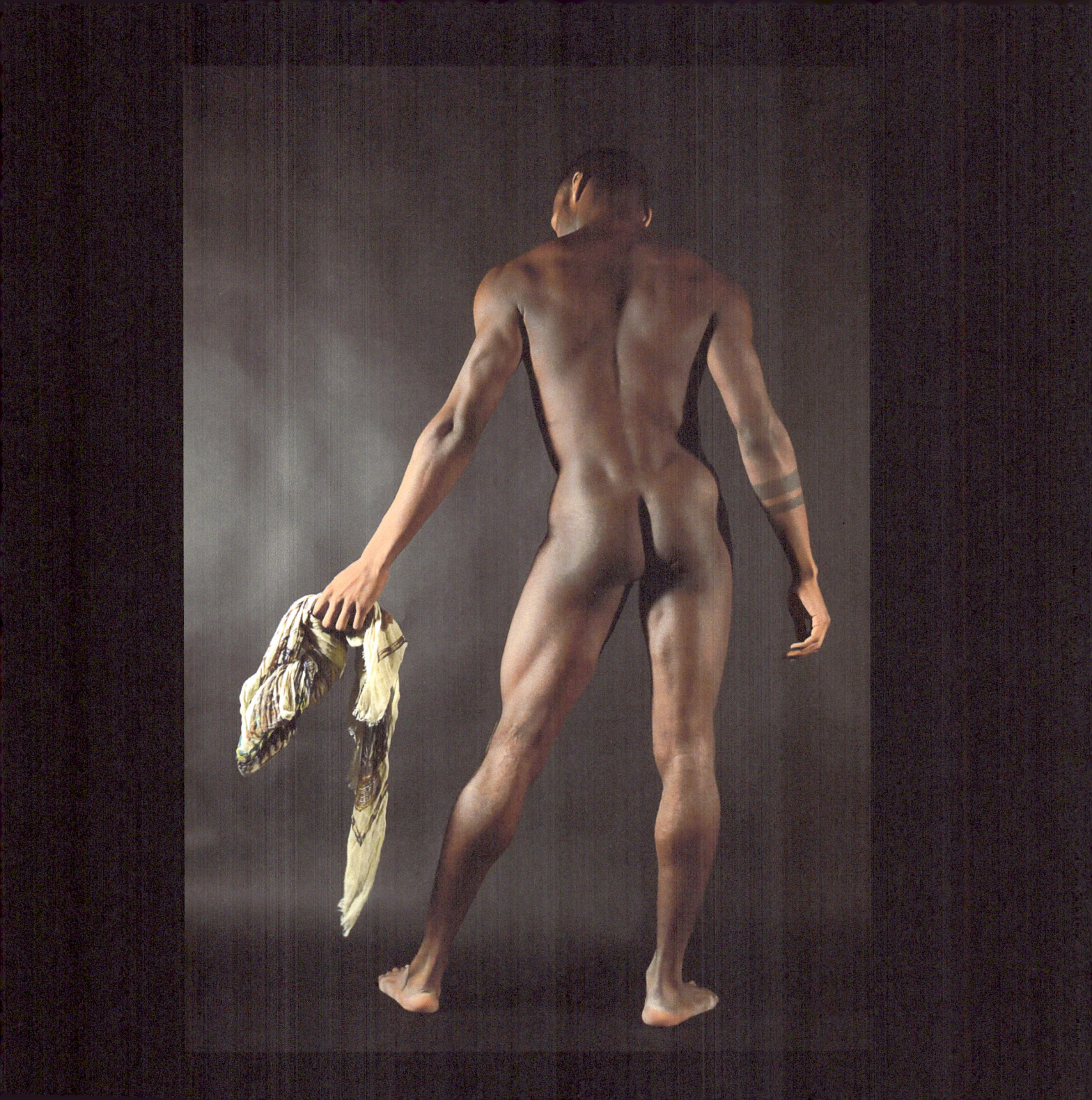

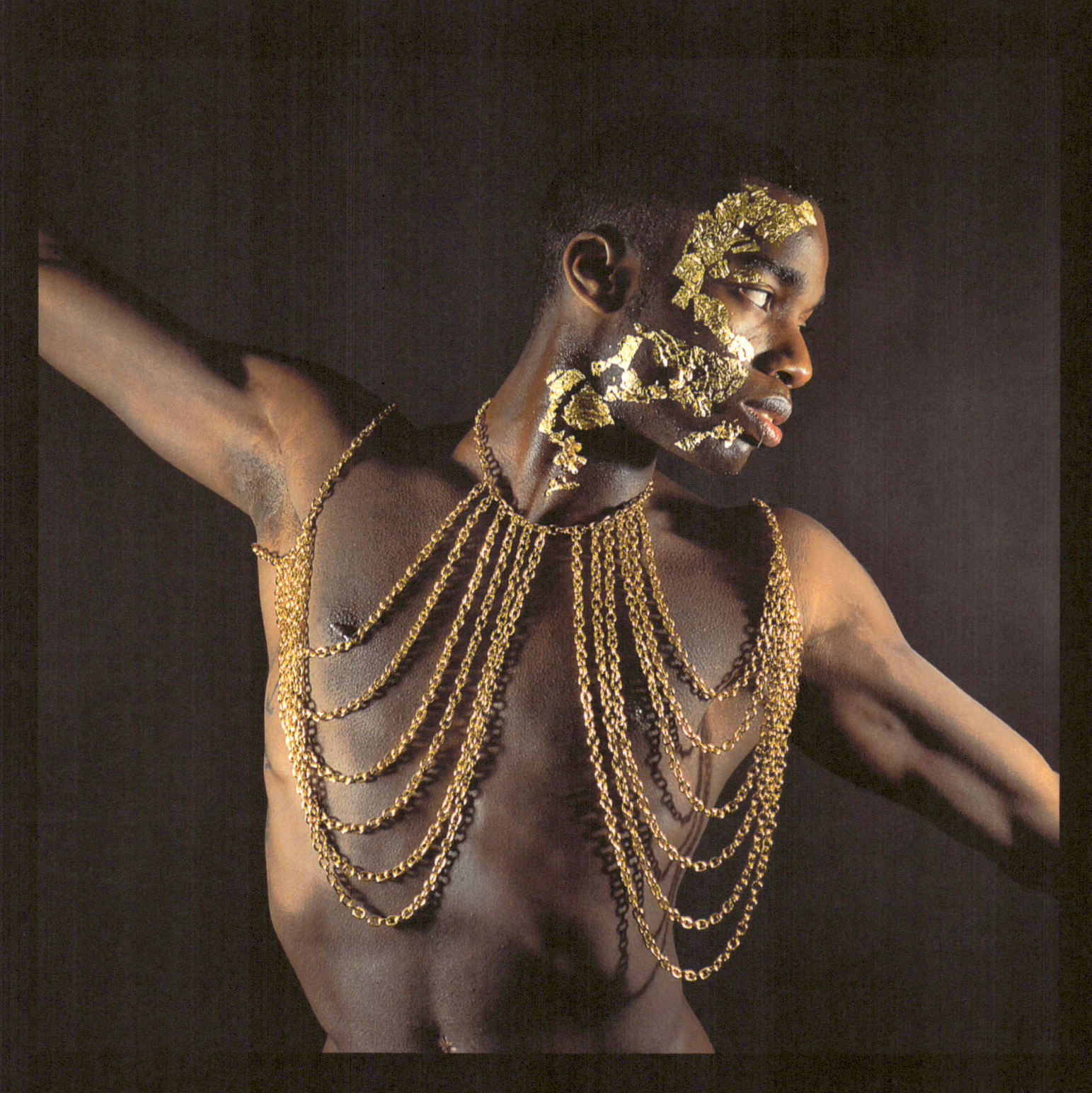

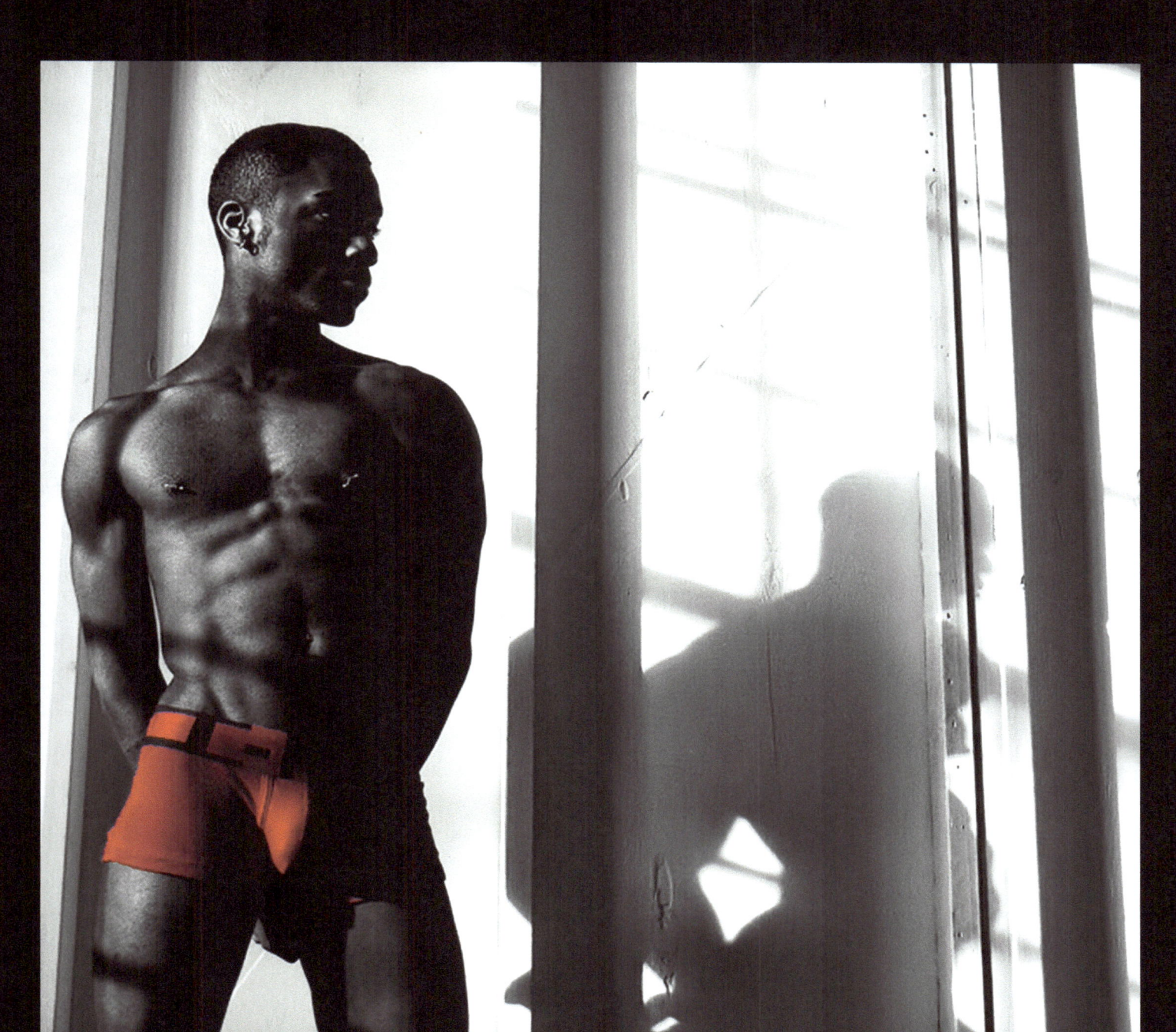

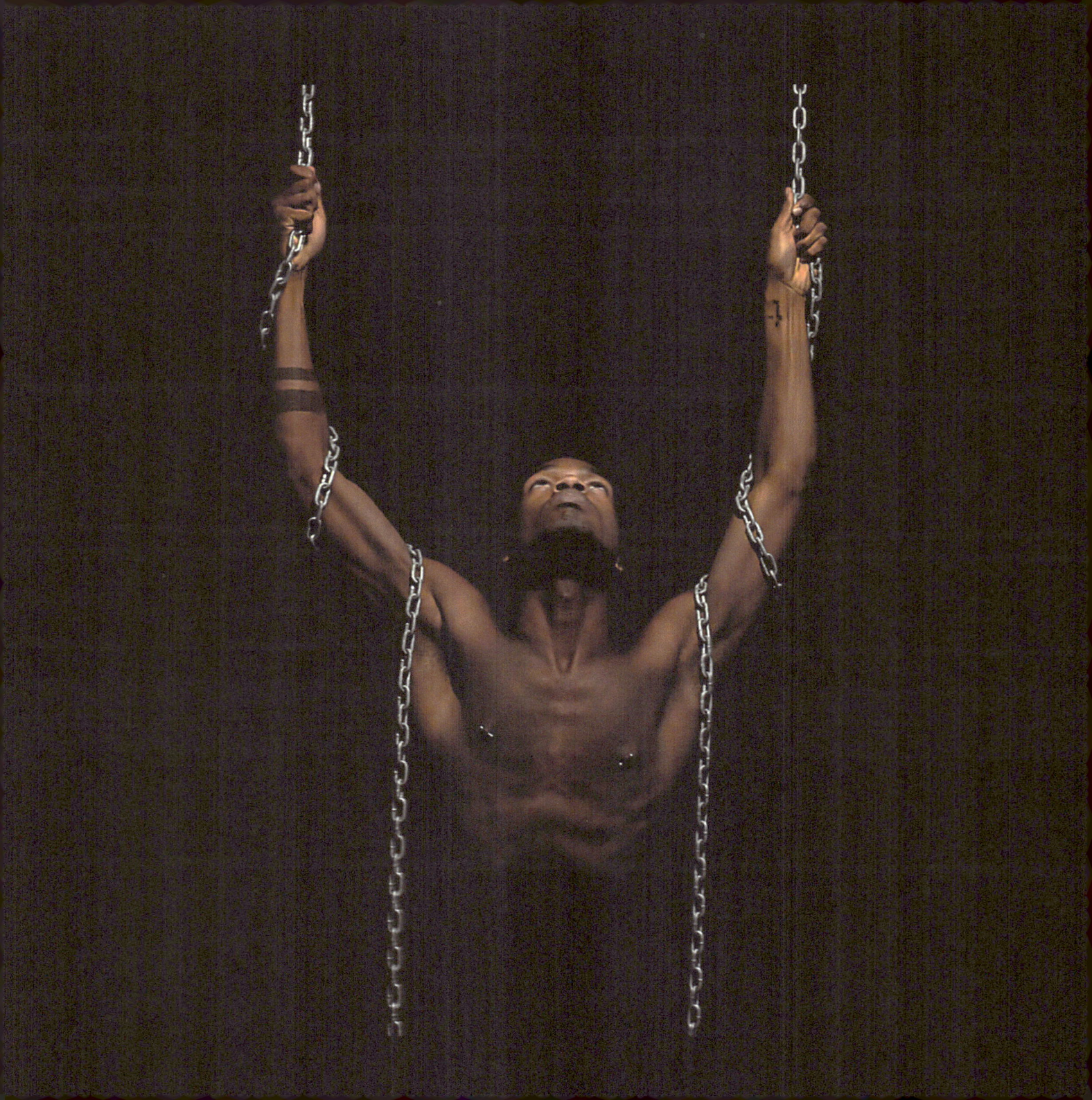

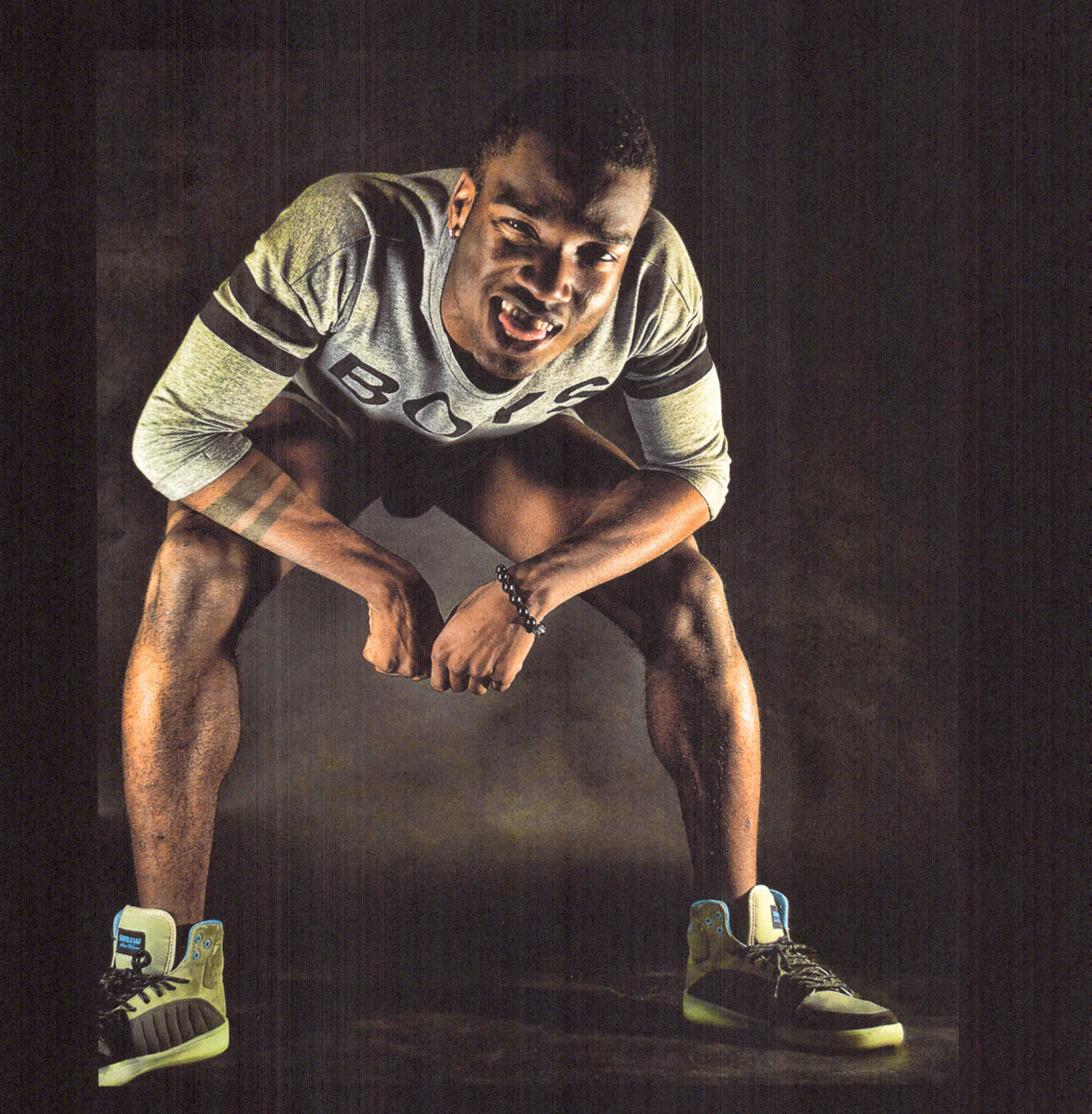

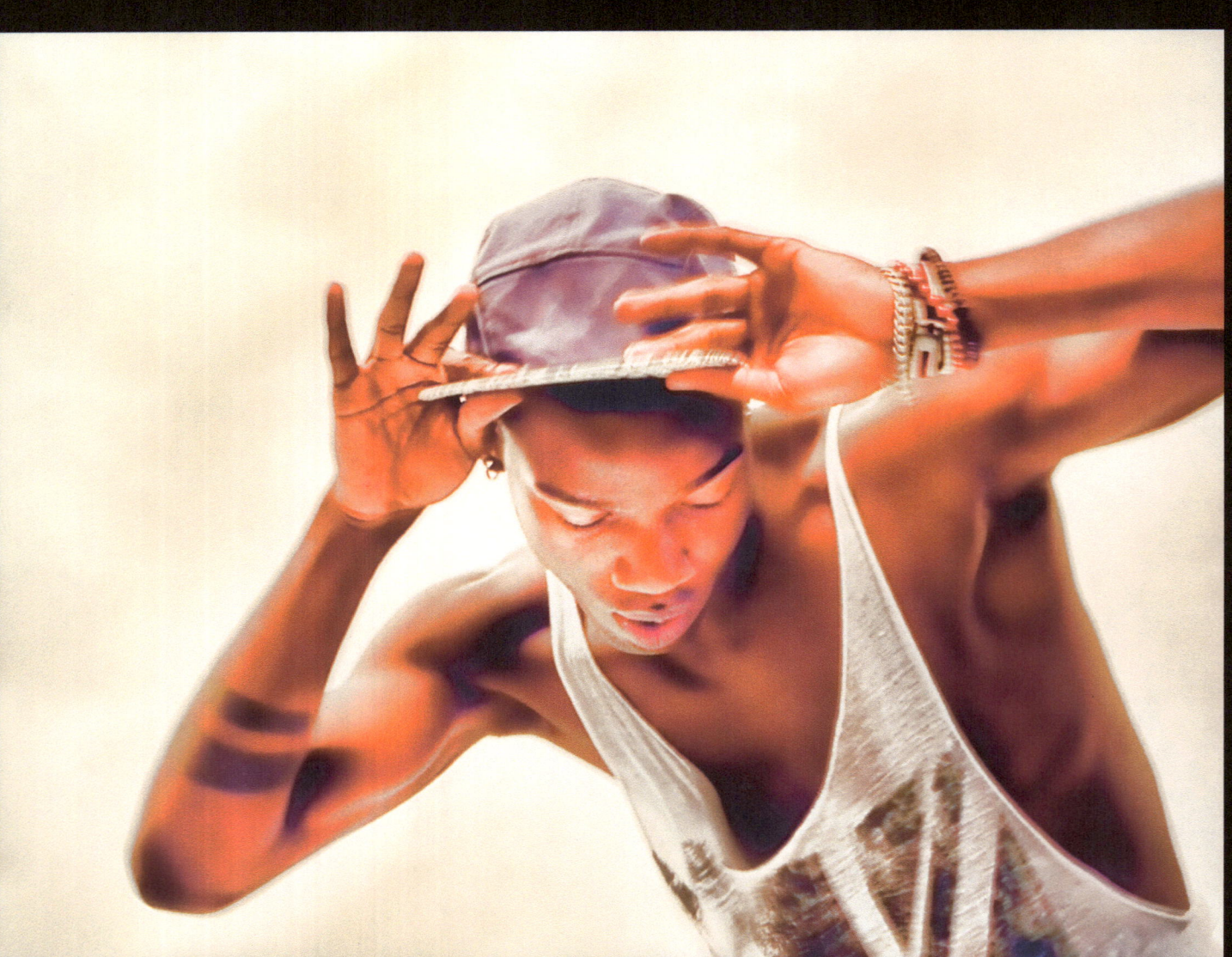

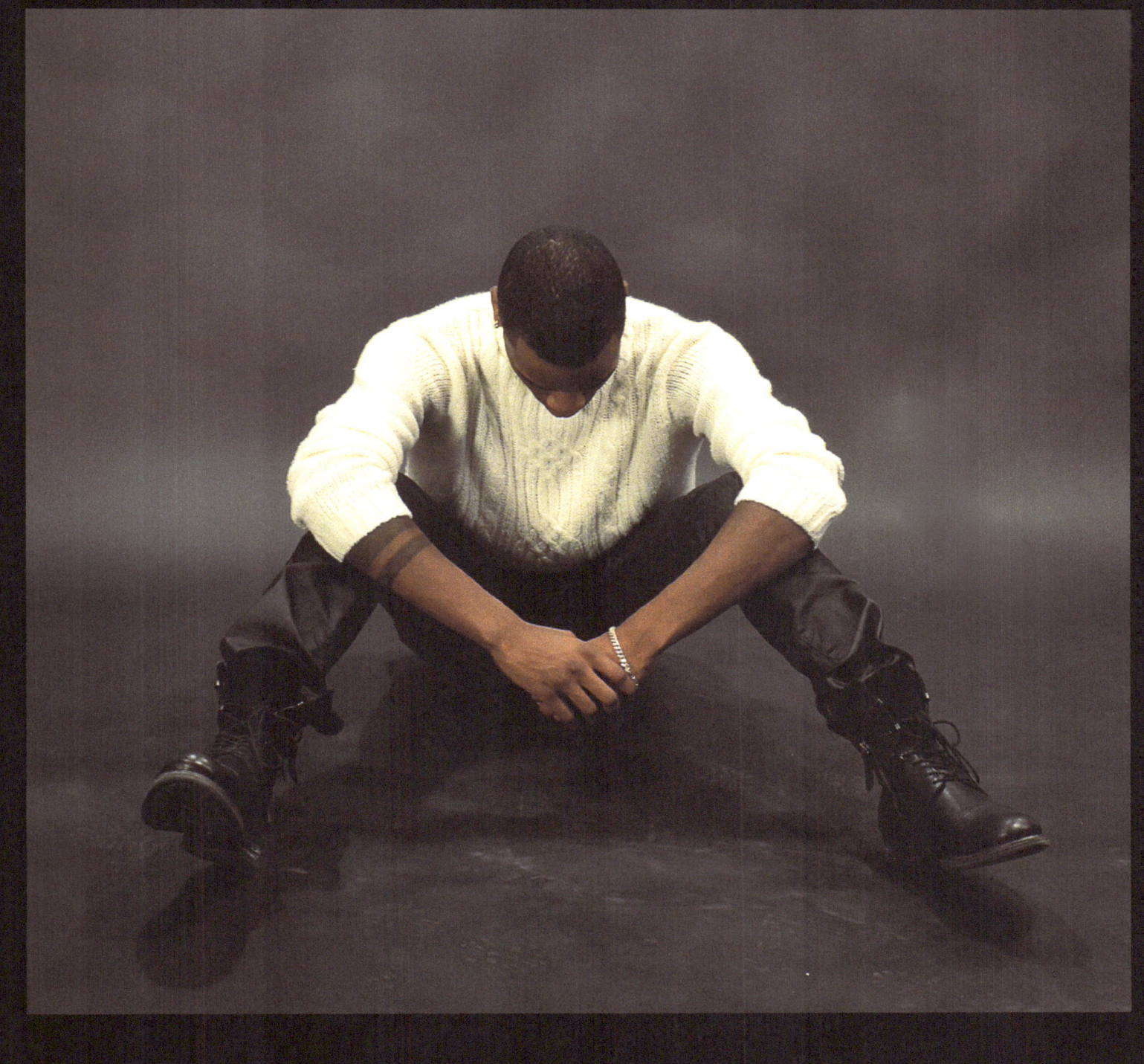

Adon-i

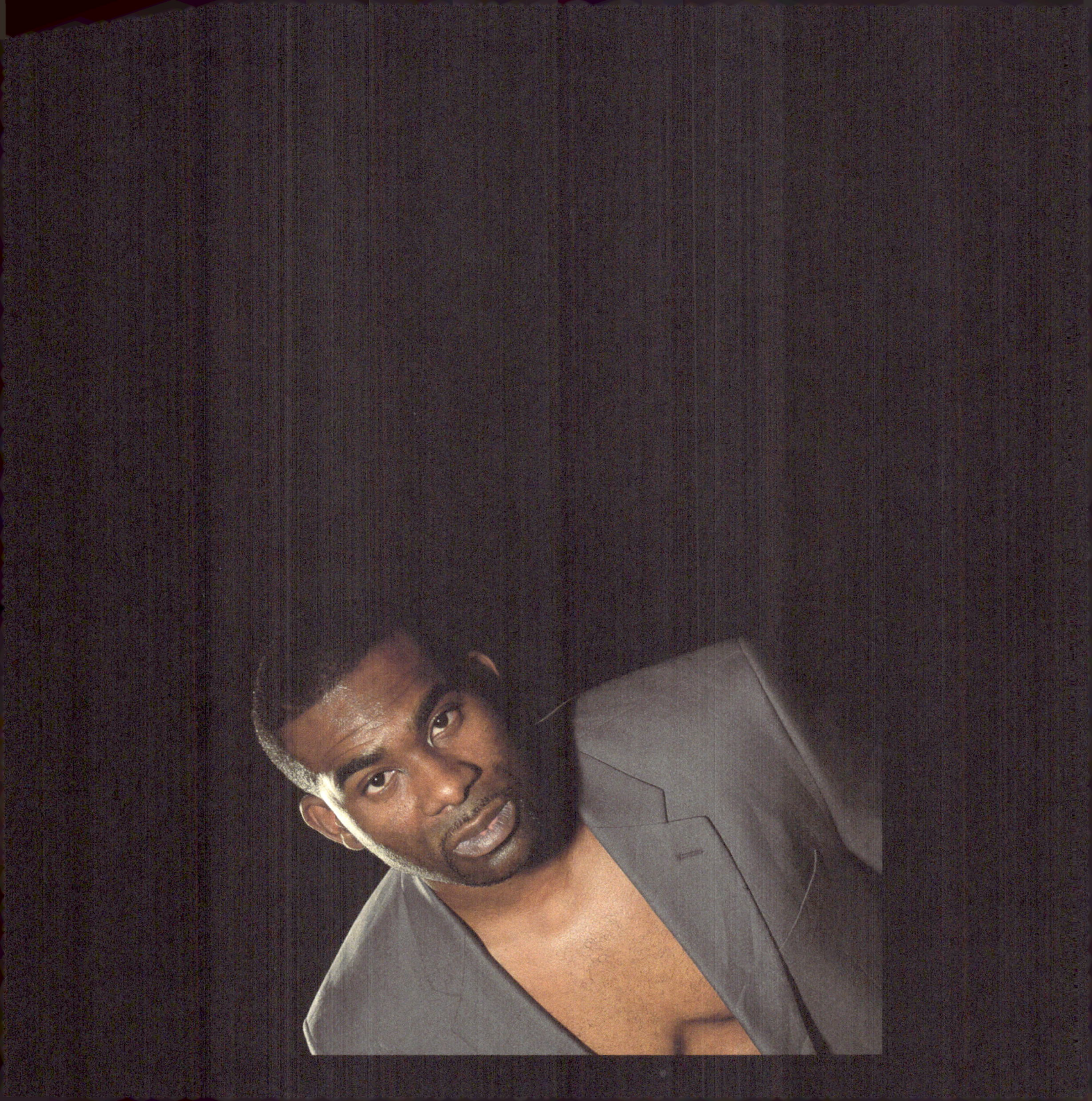

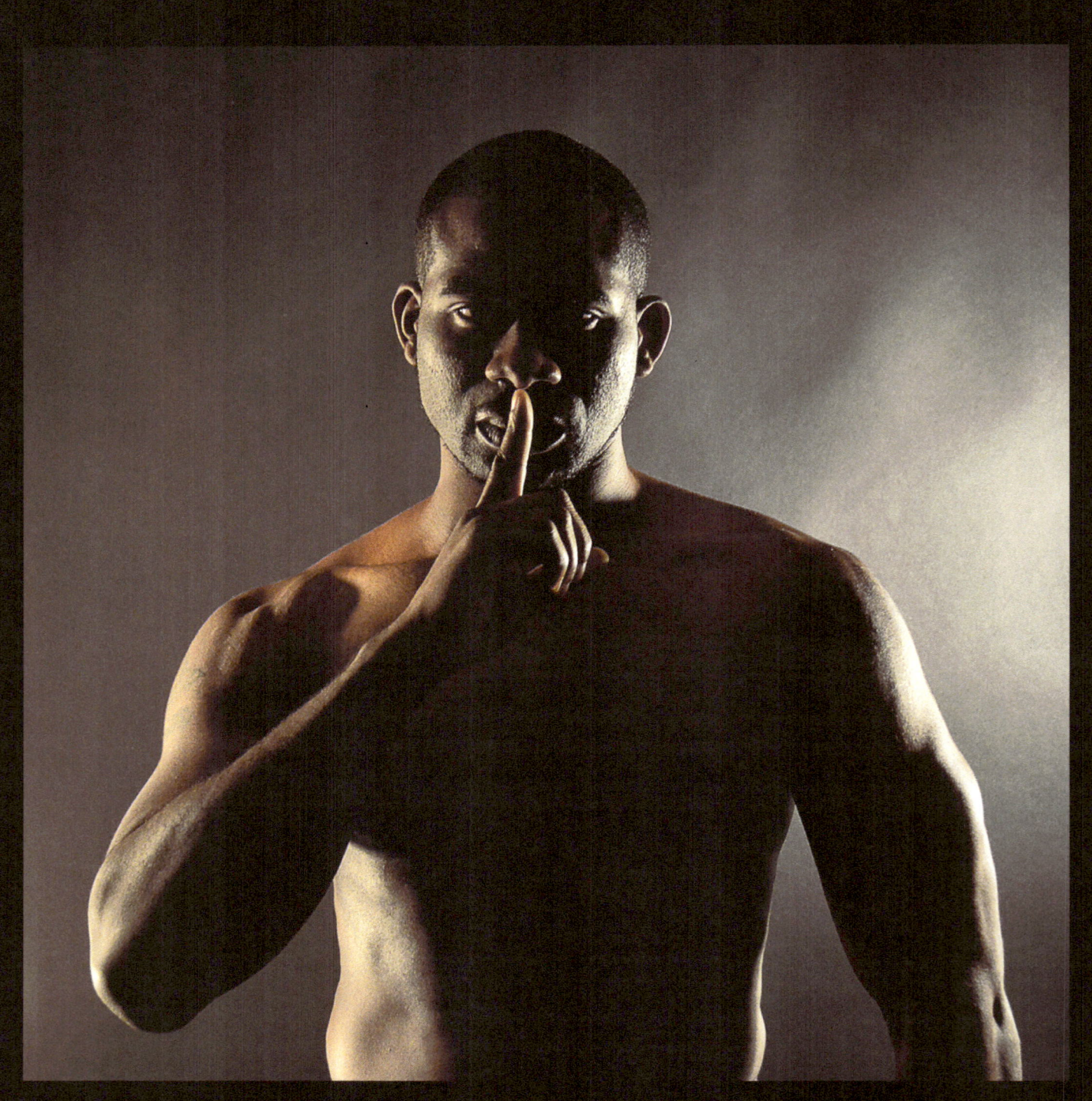

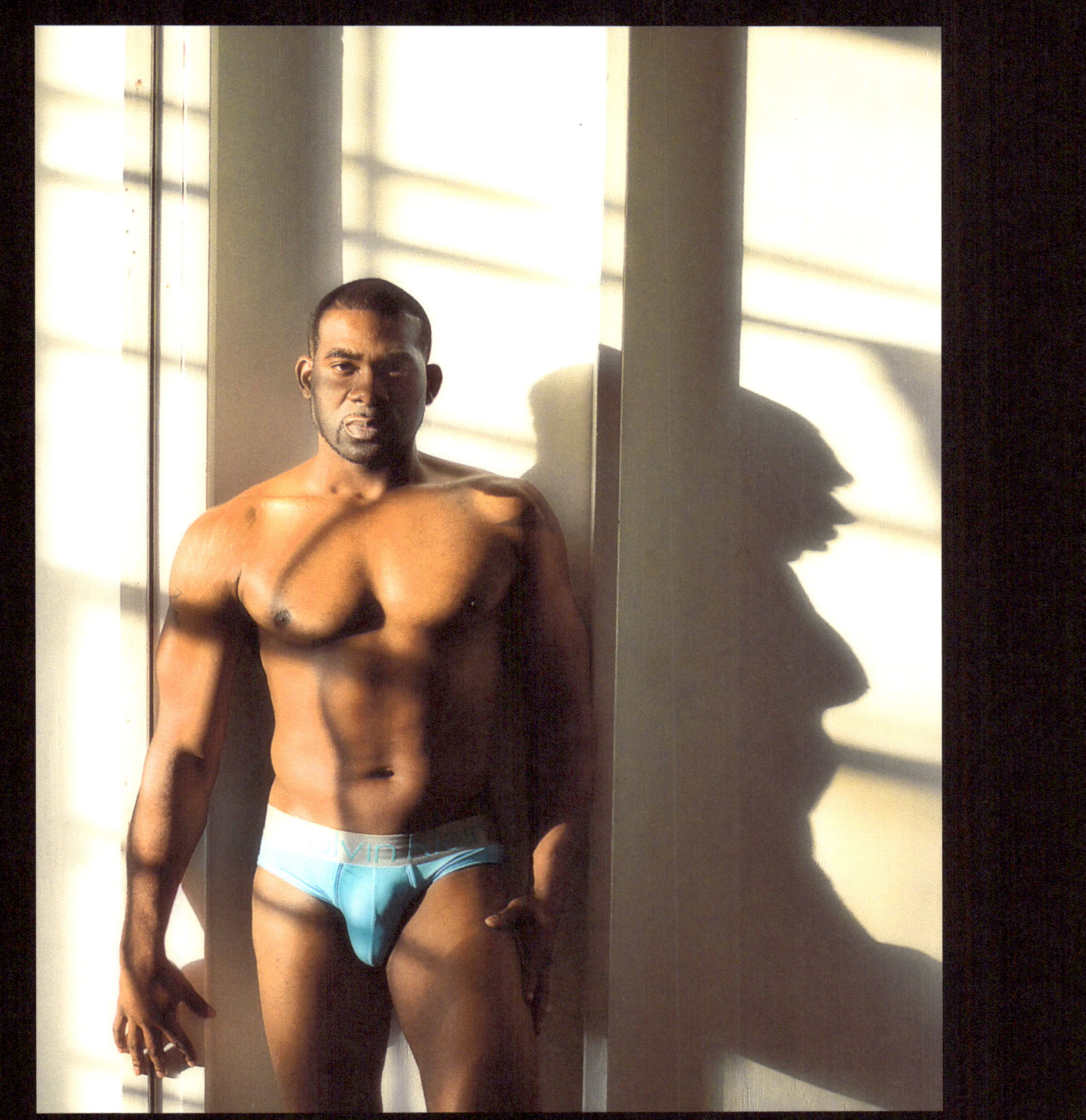

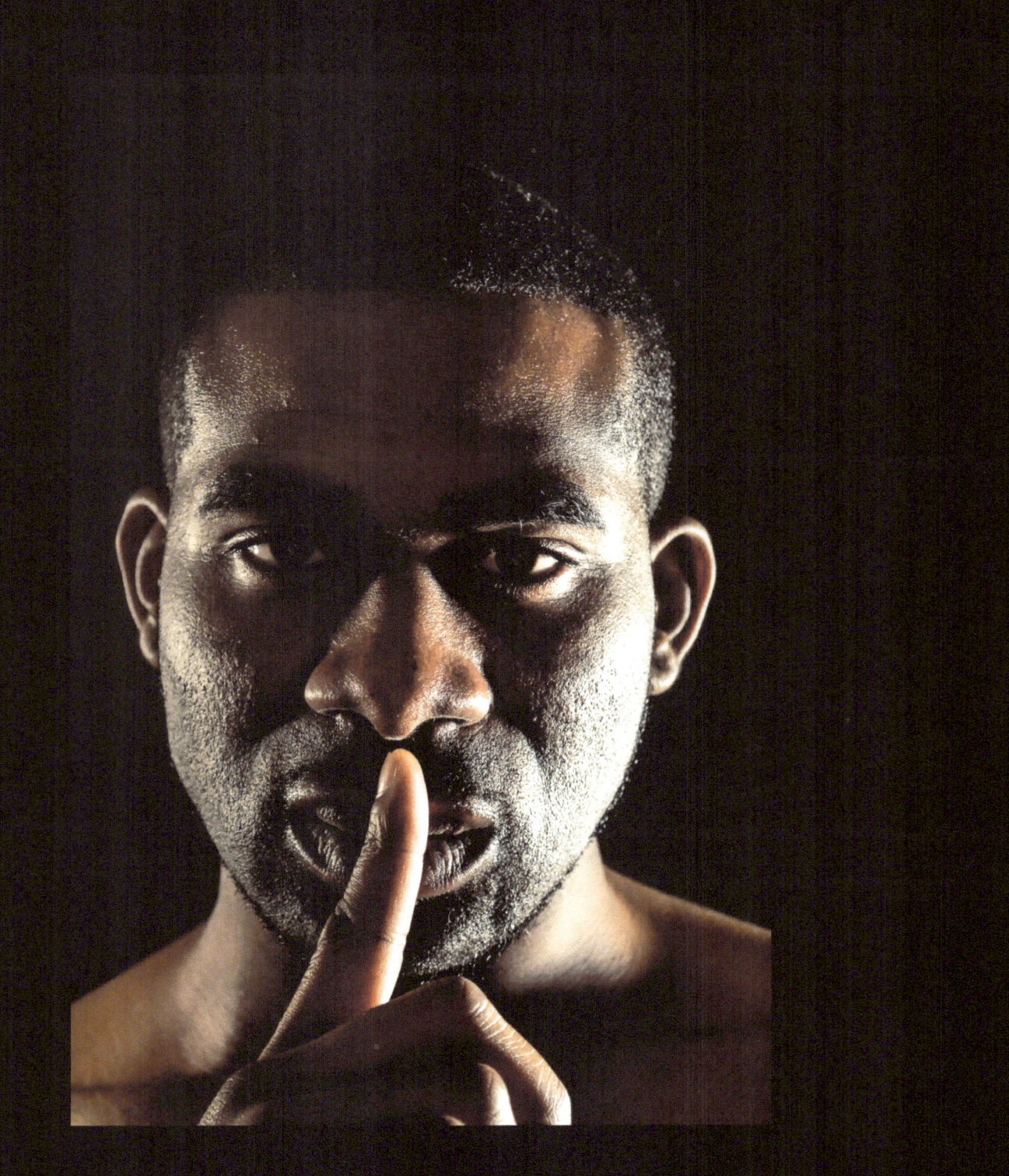

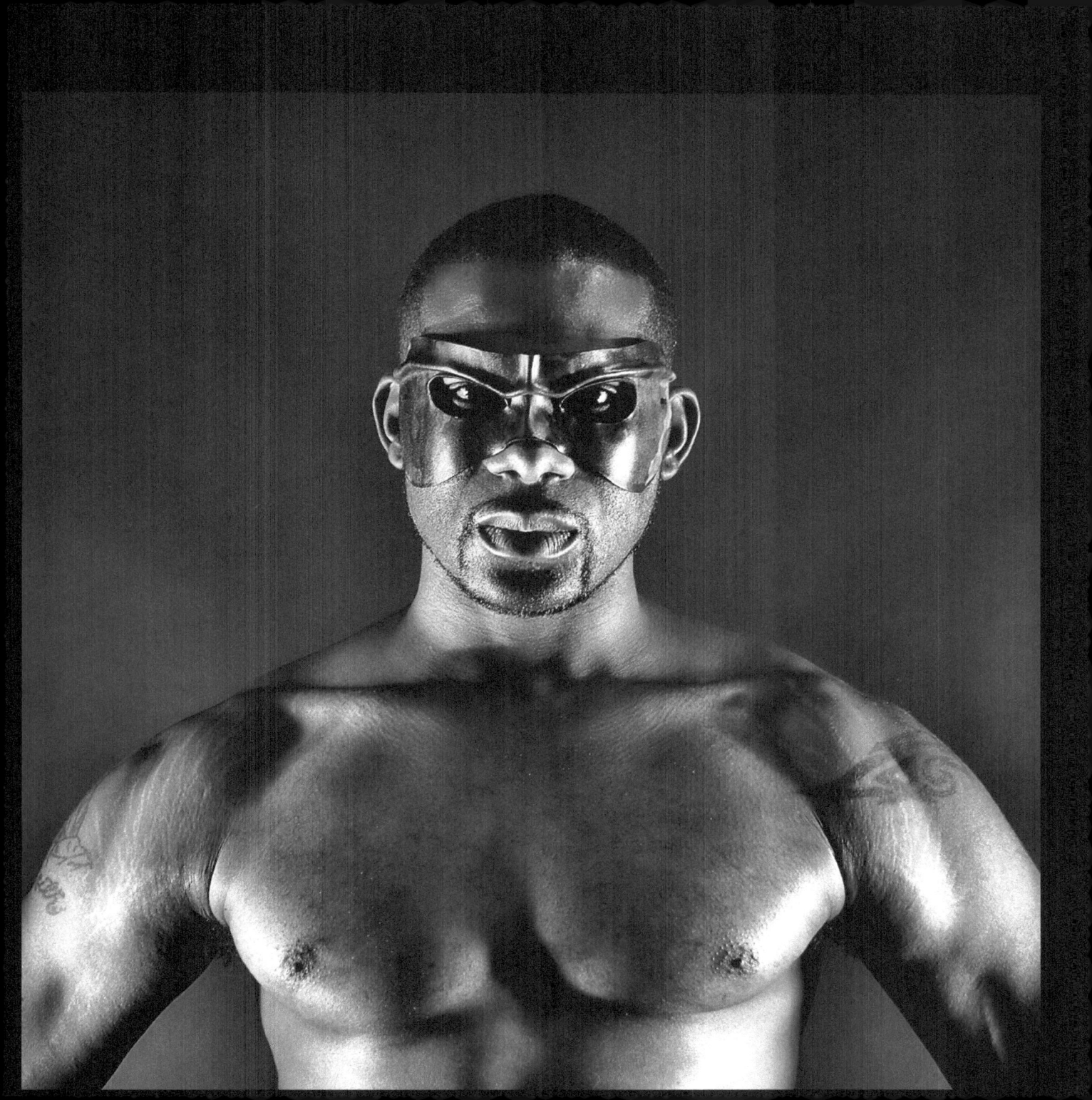

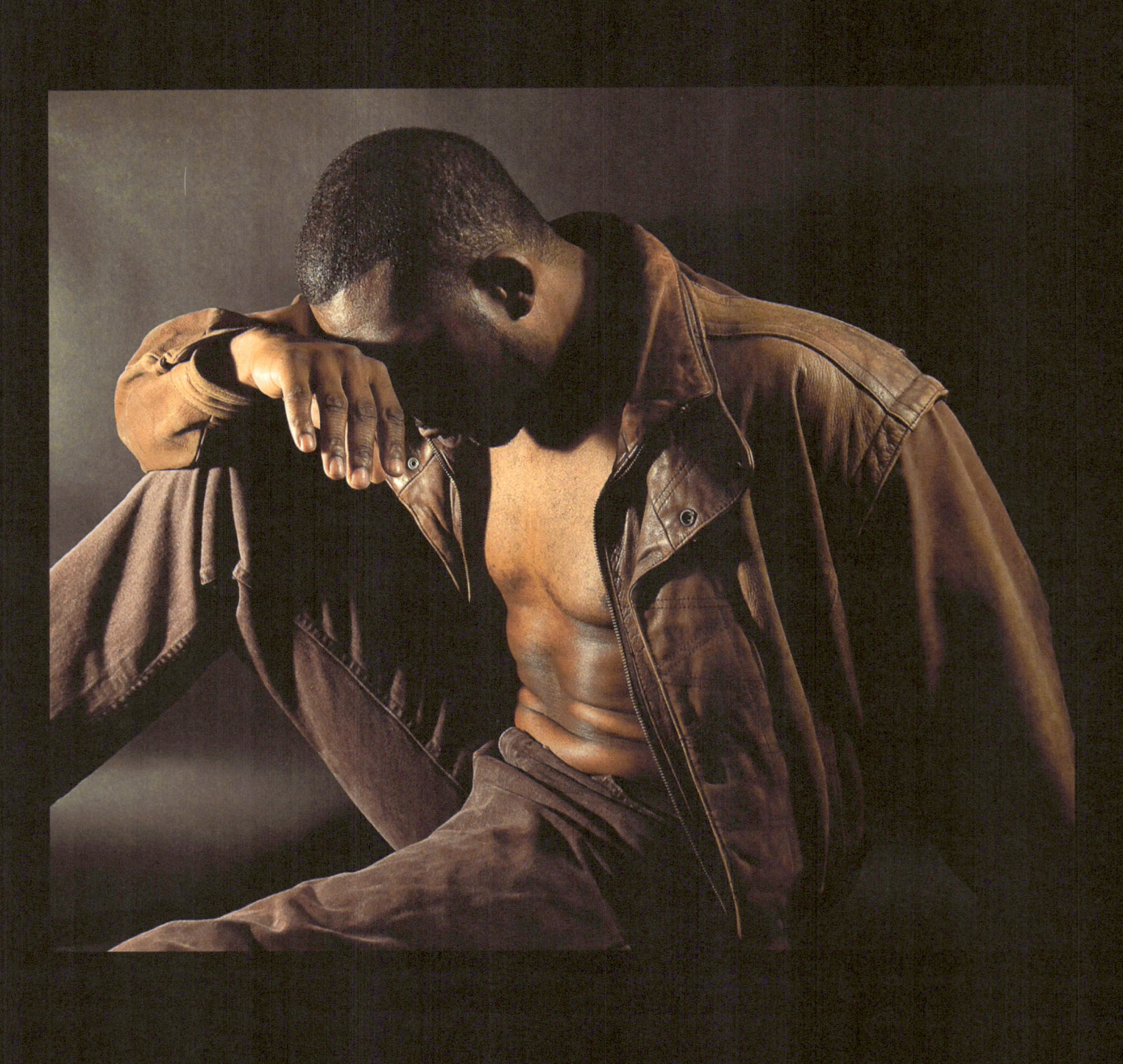

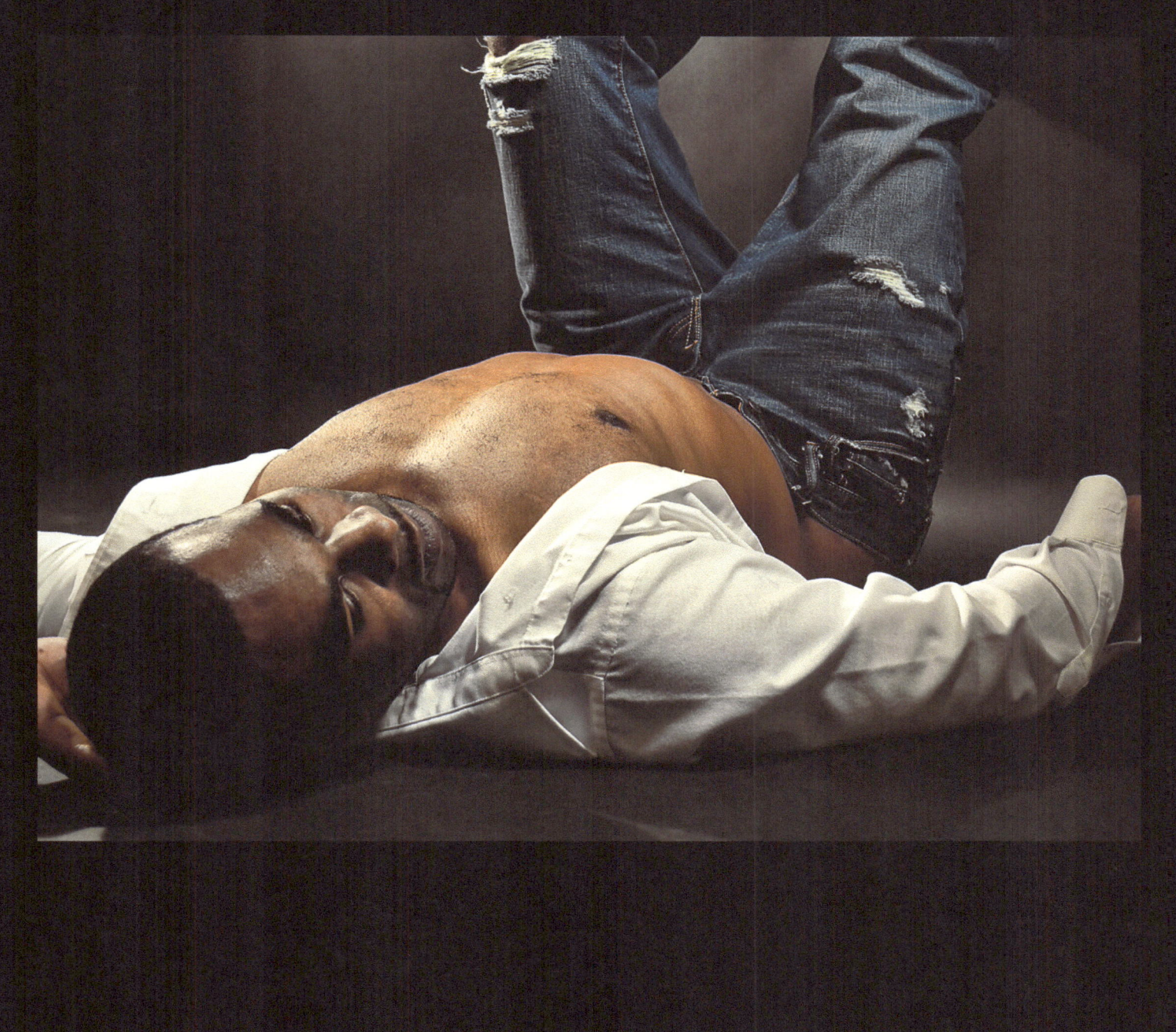

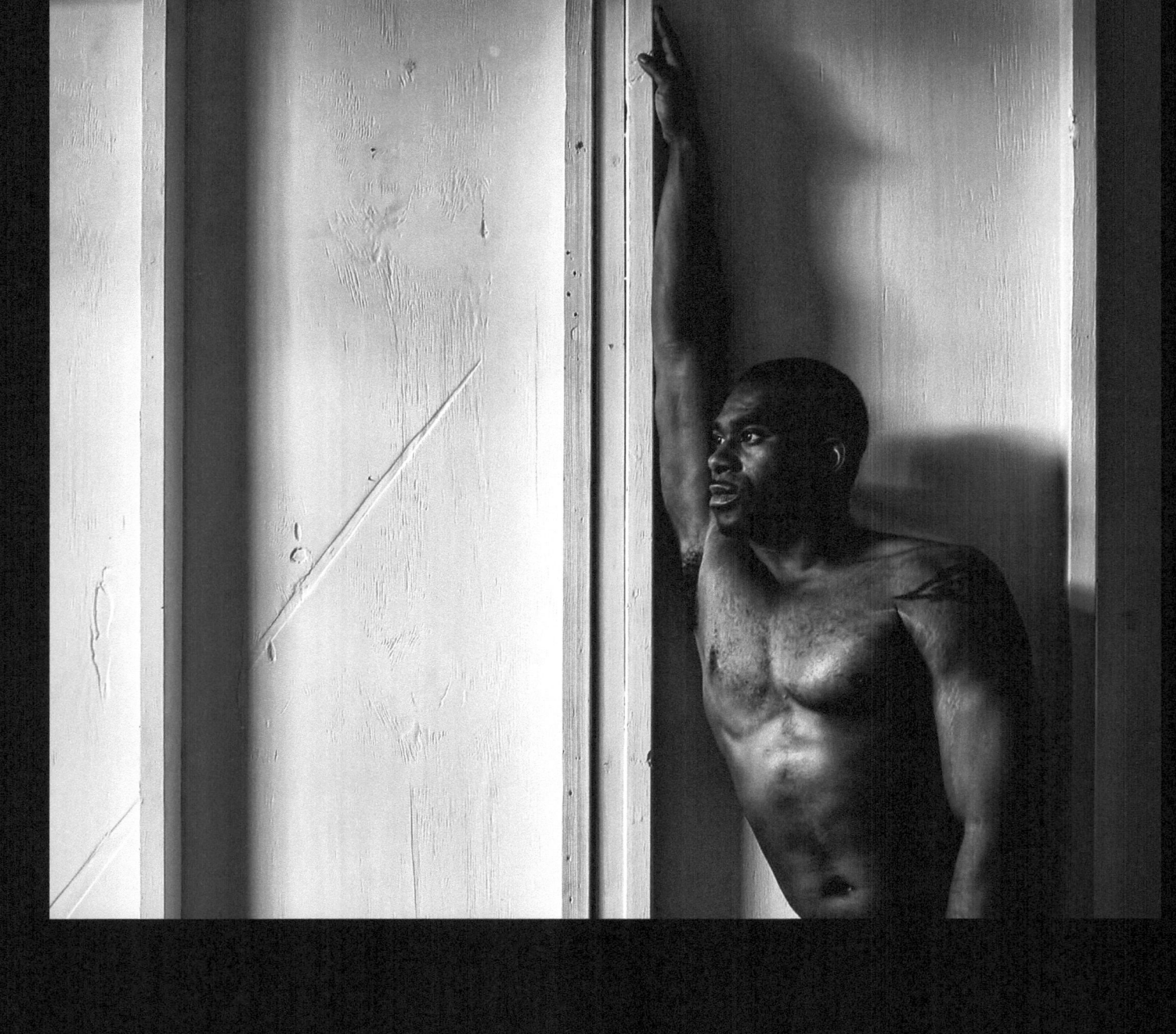

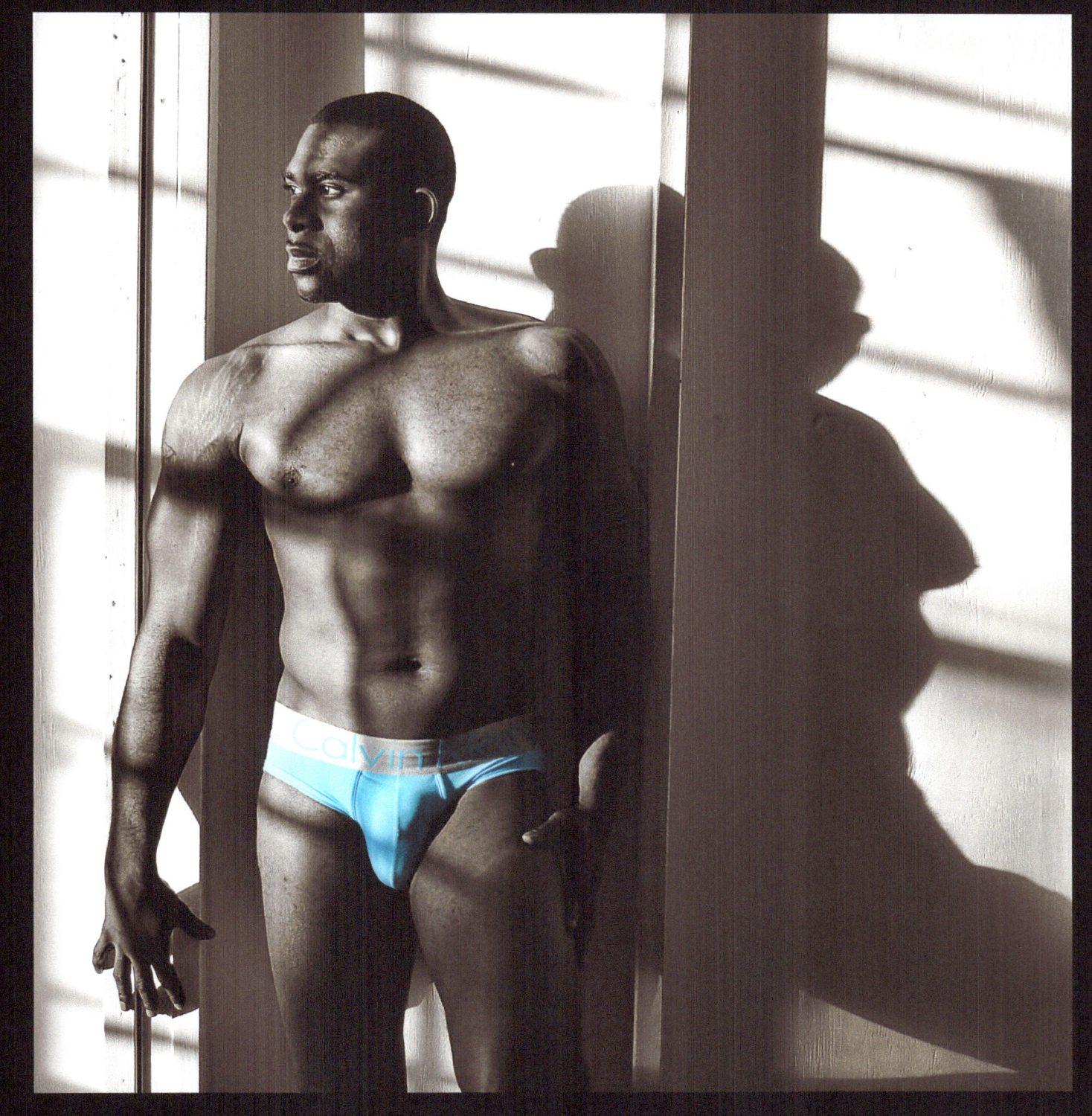

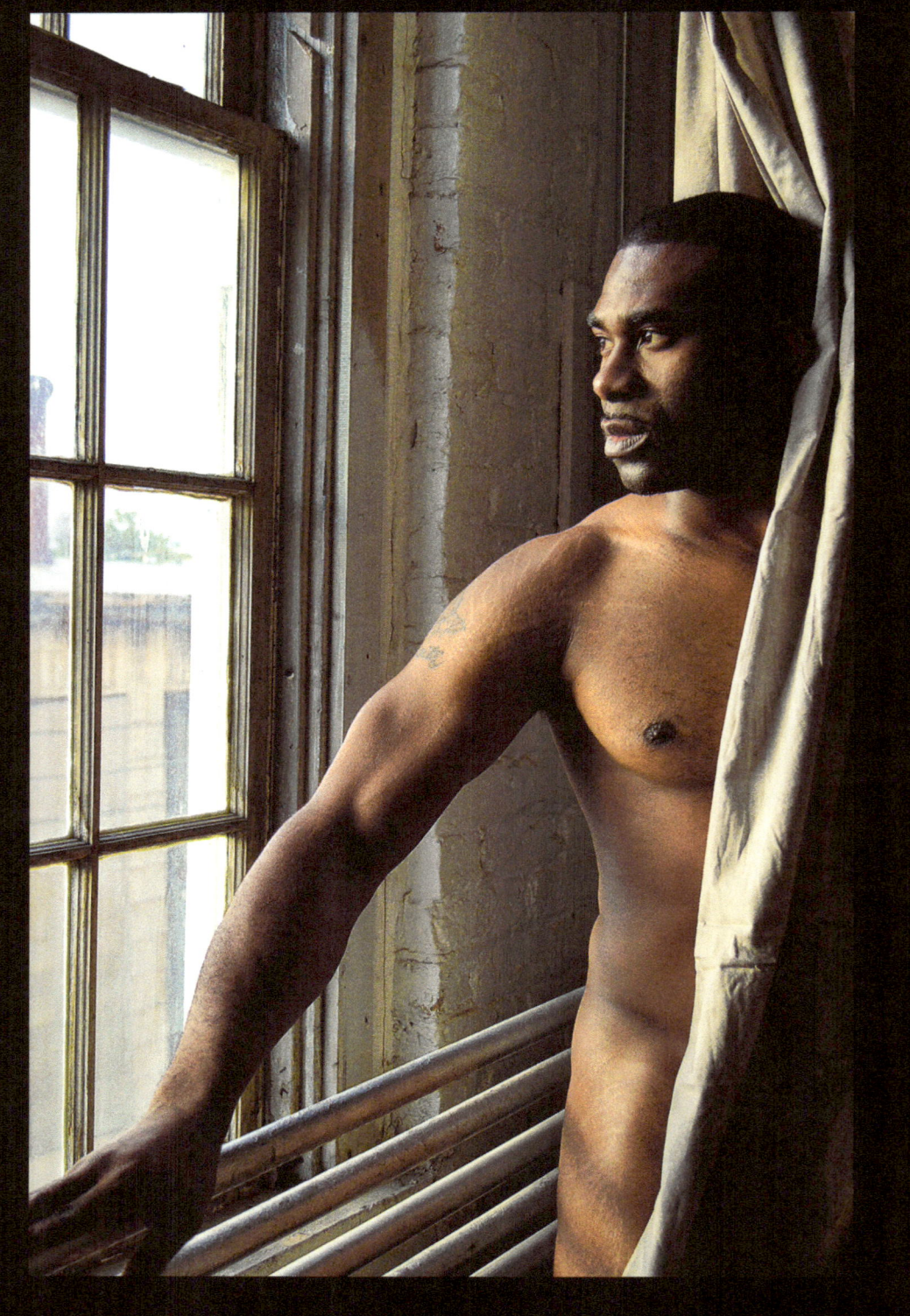

Devon

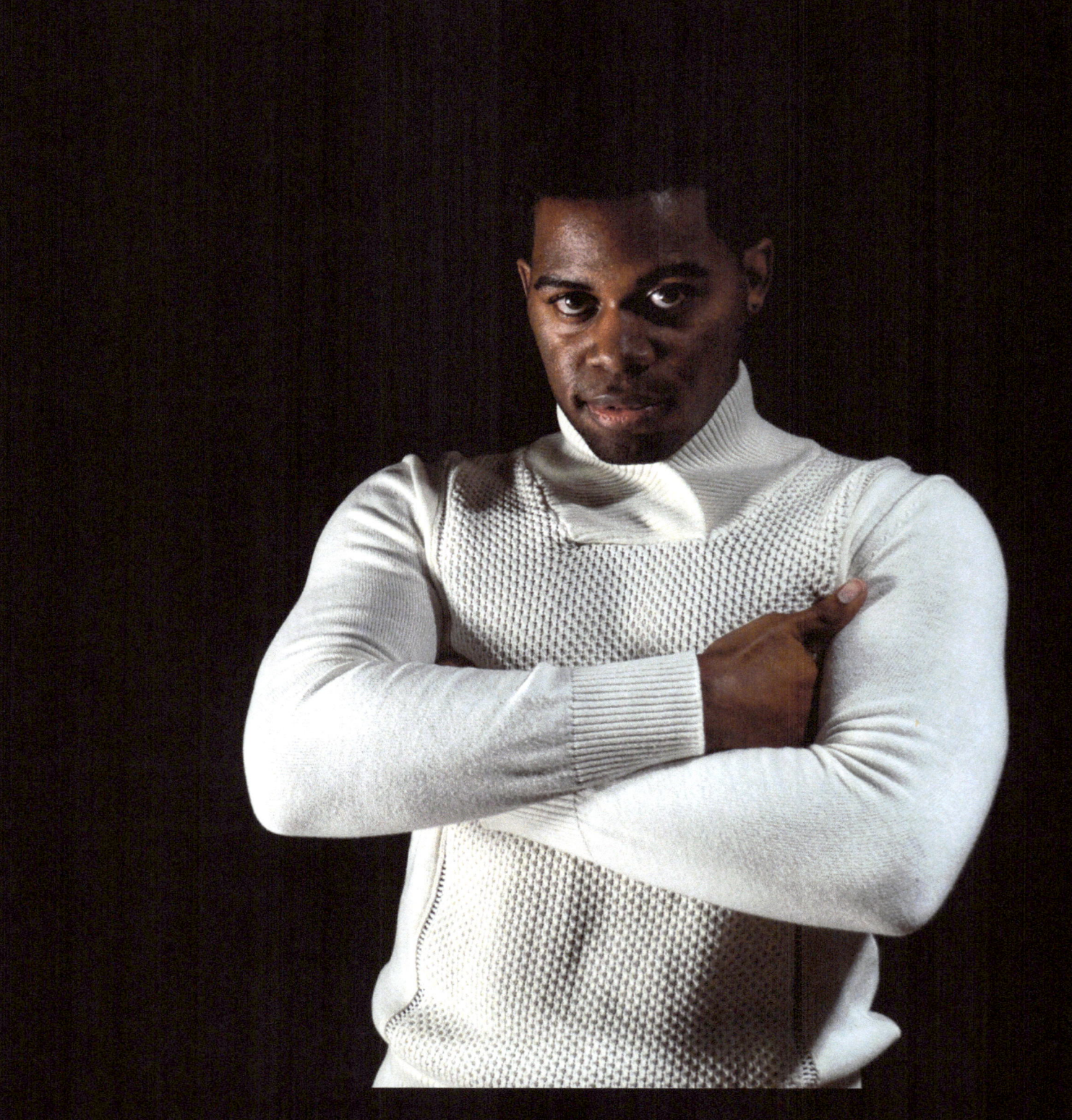

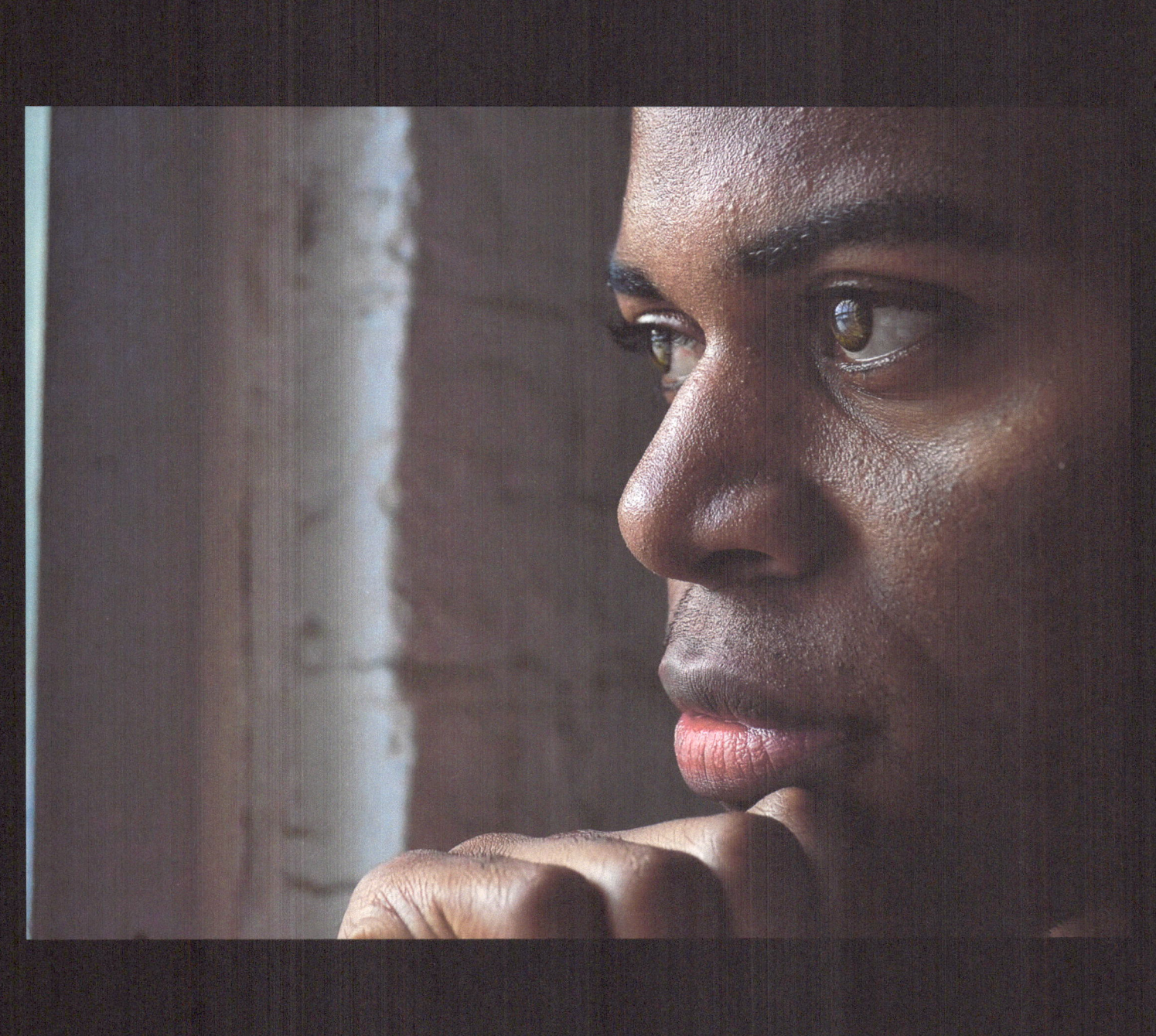

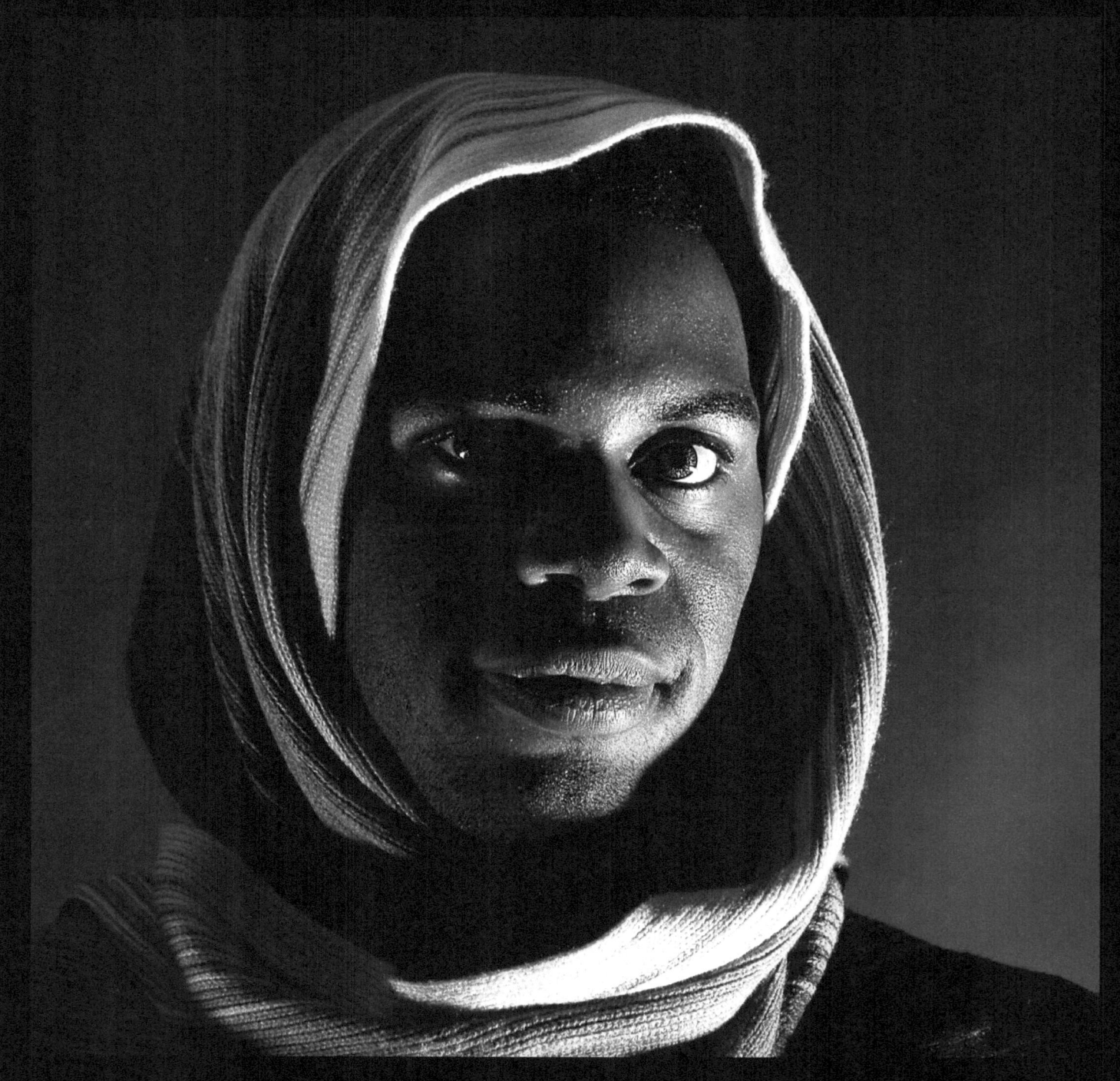

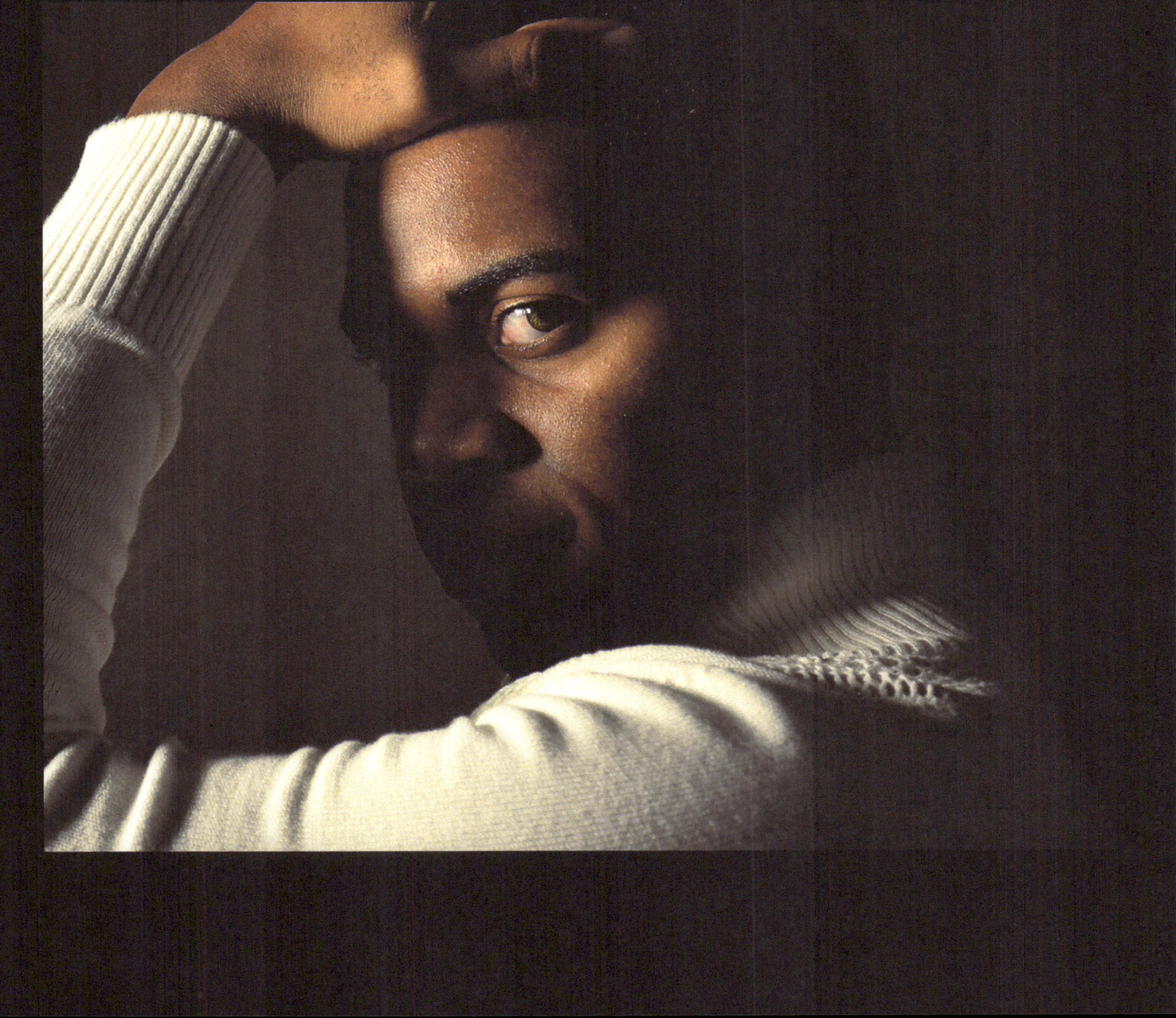

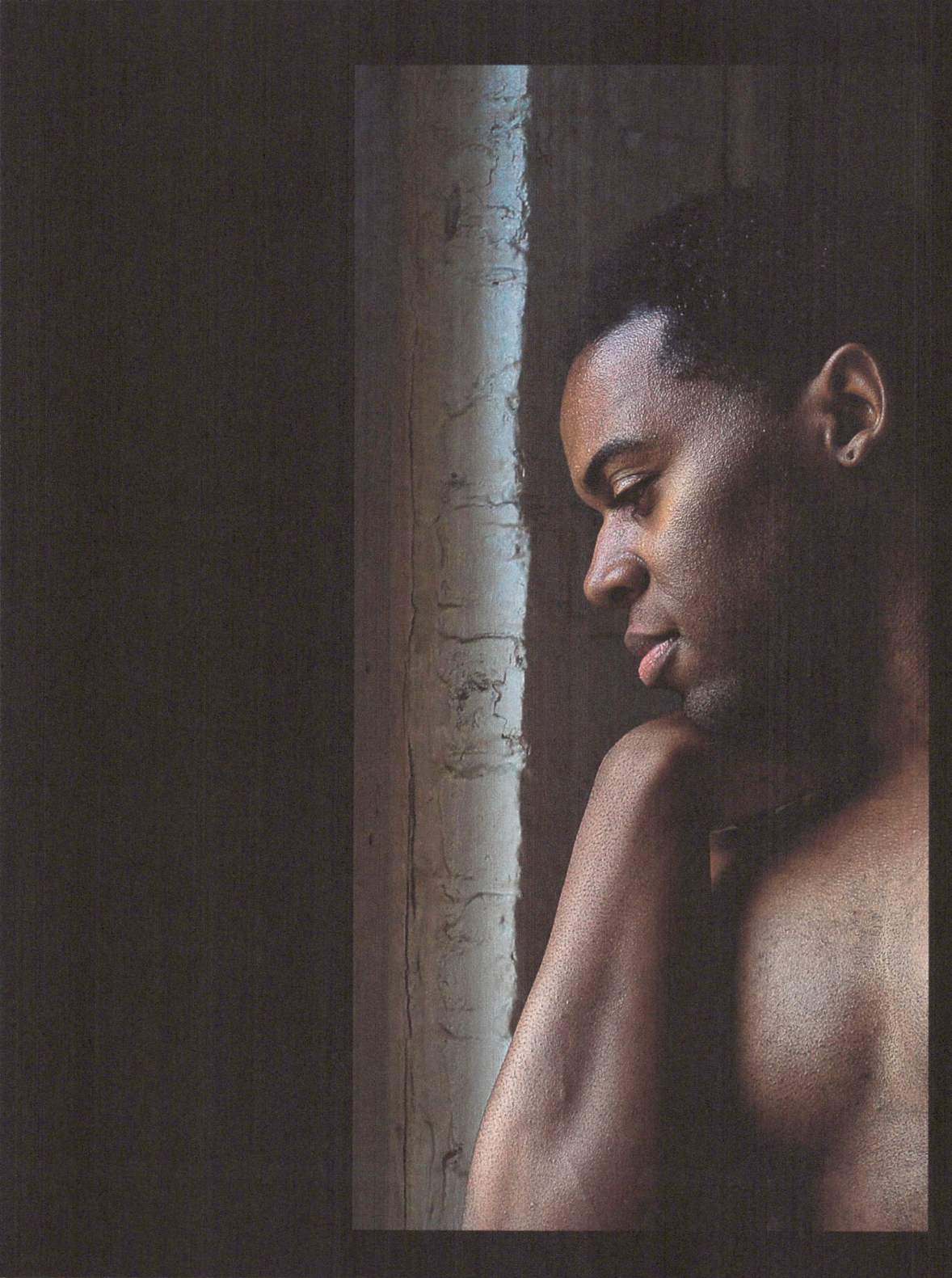

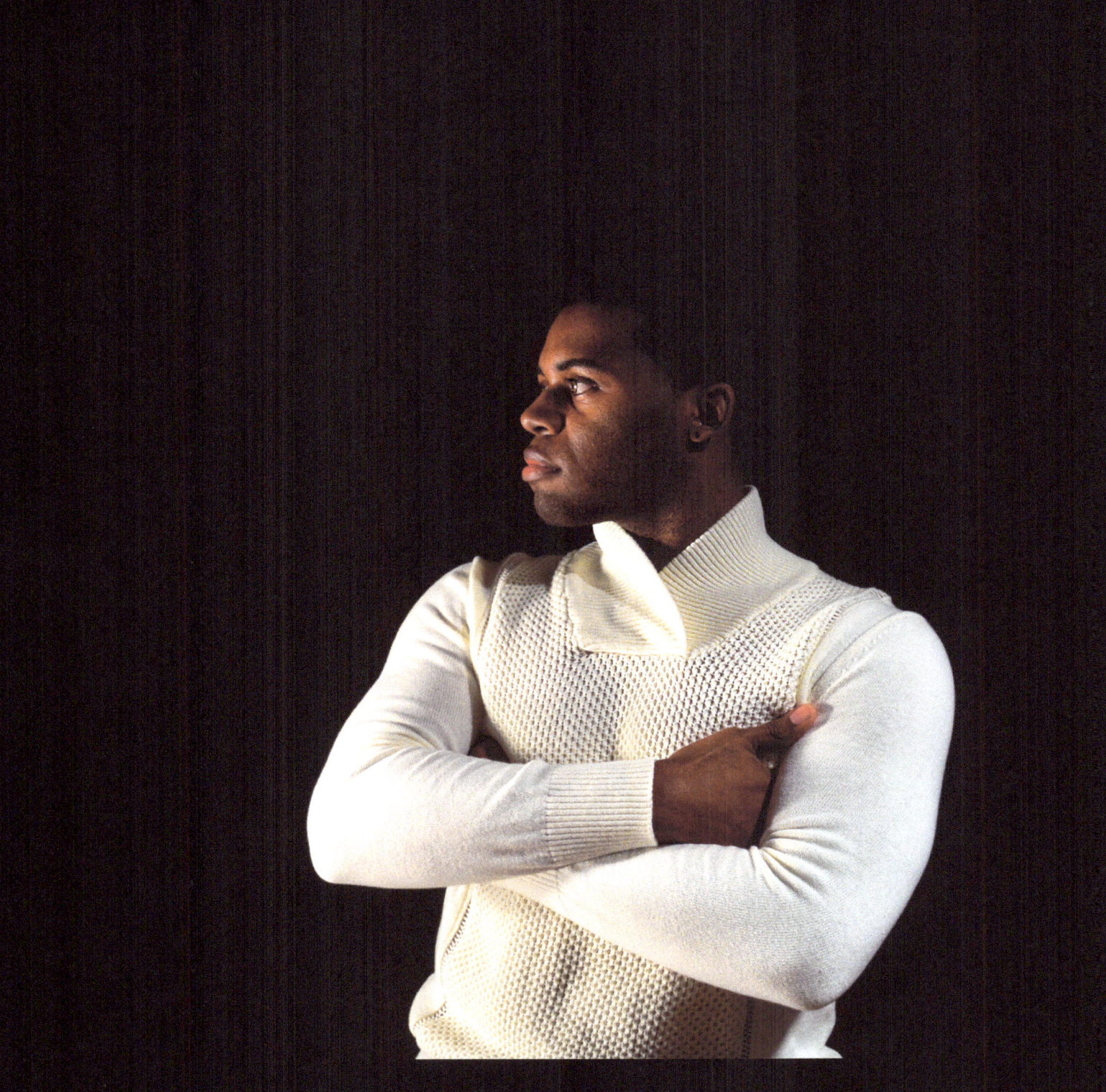

Monroe

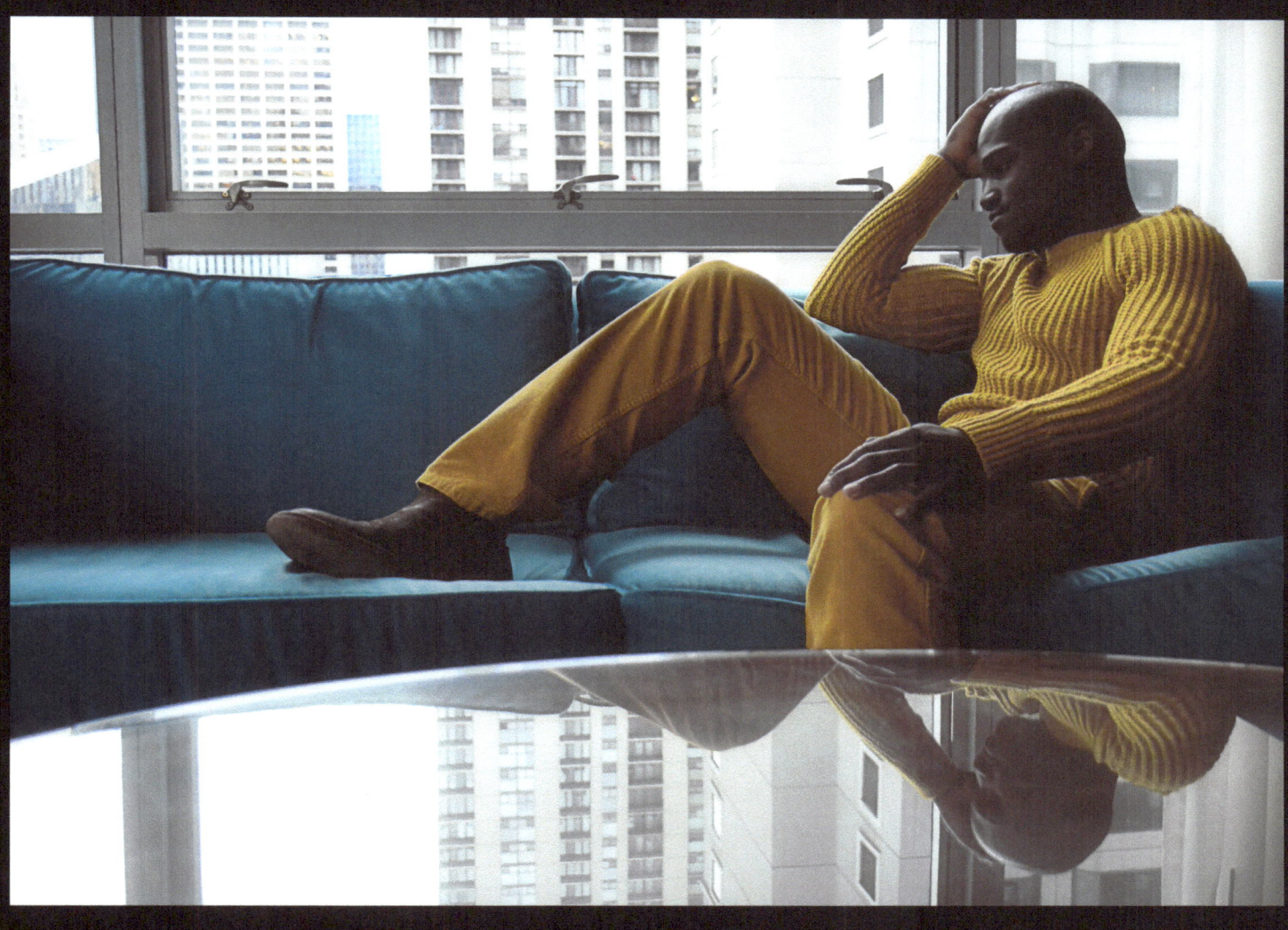

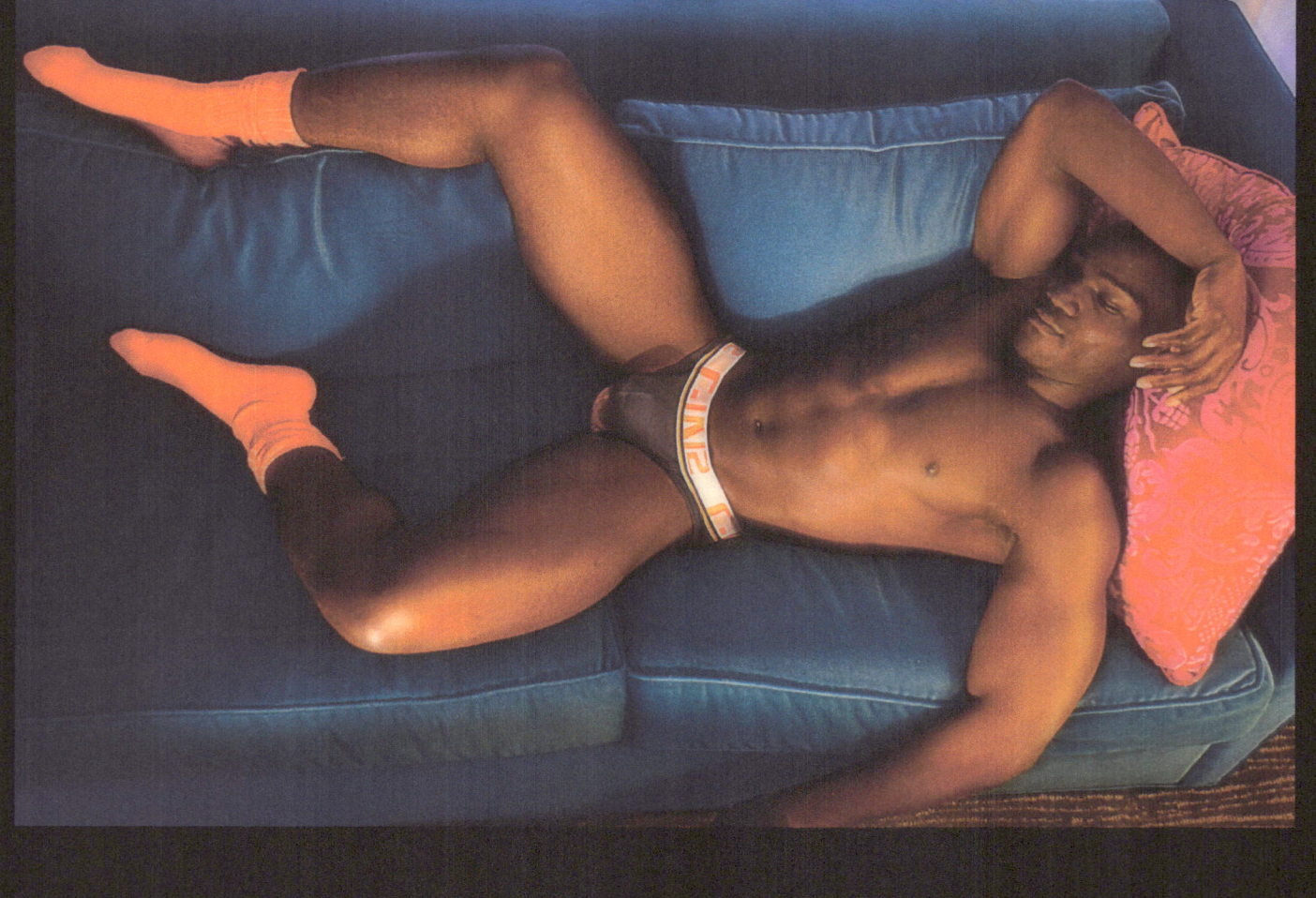

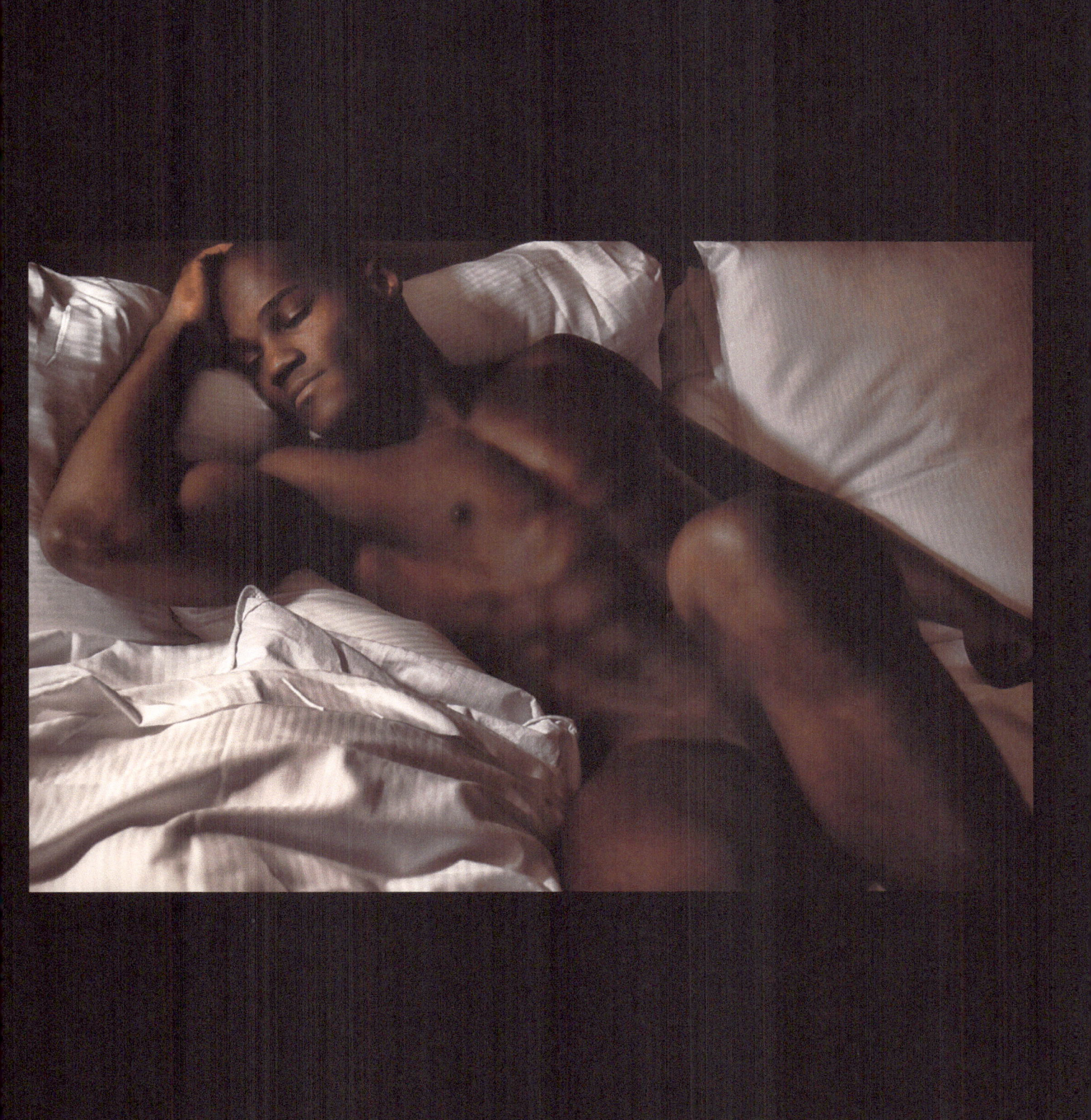

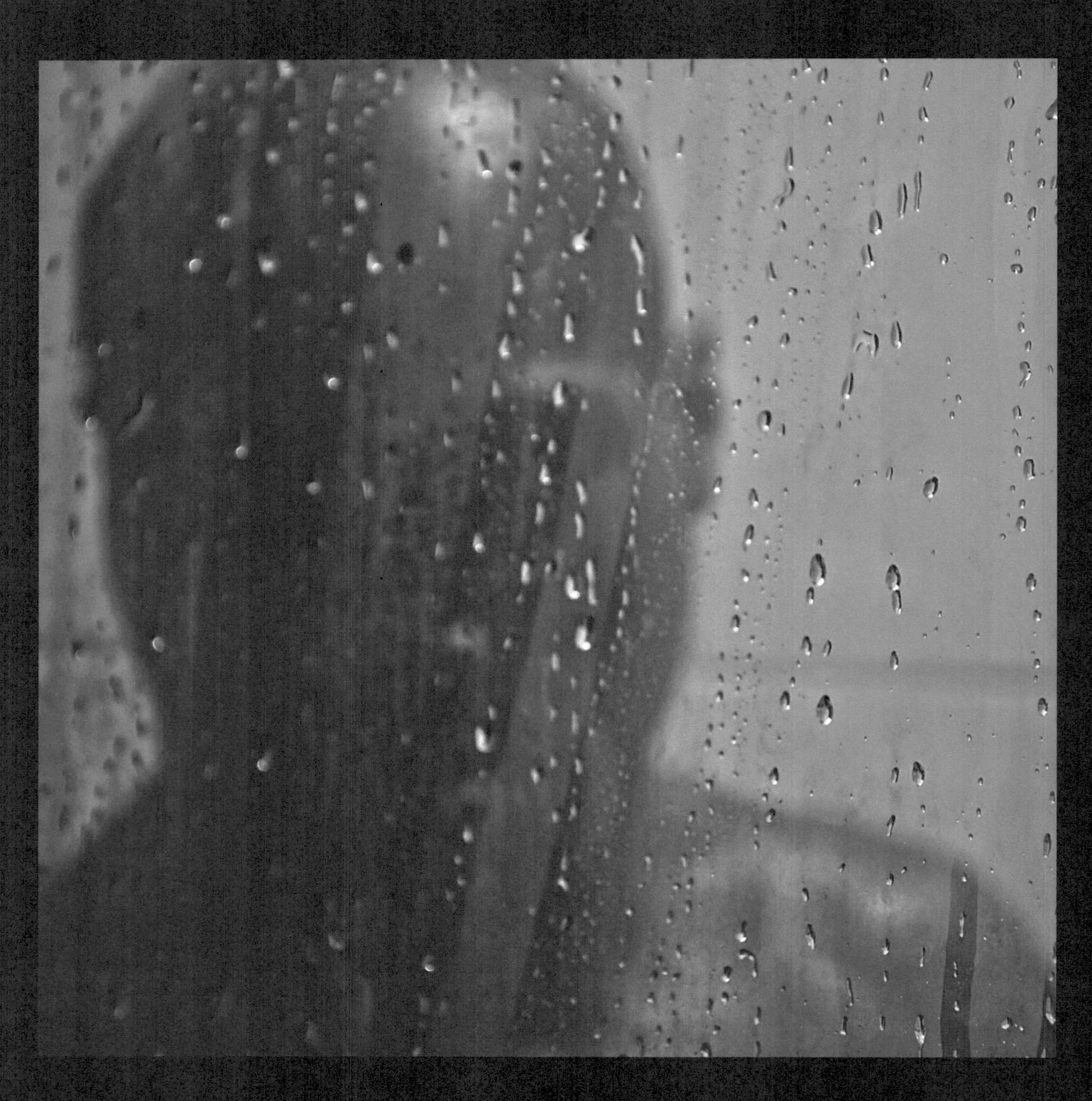

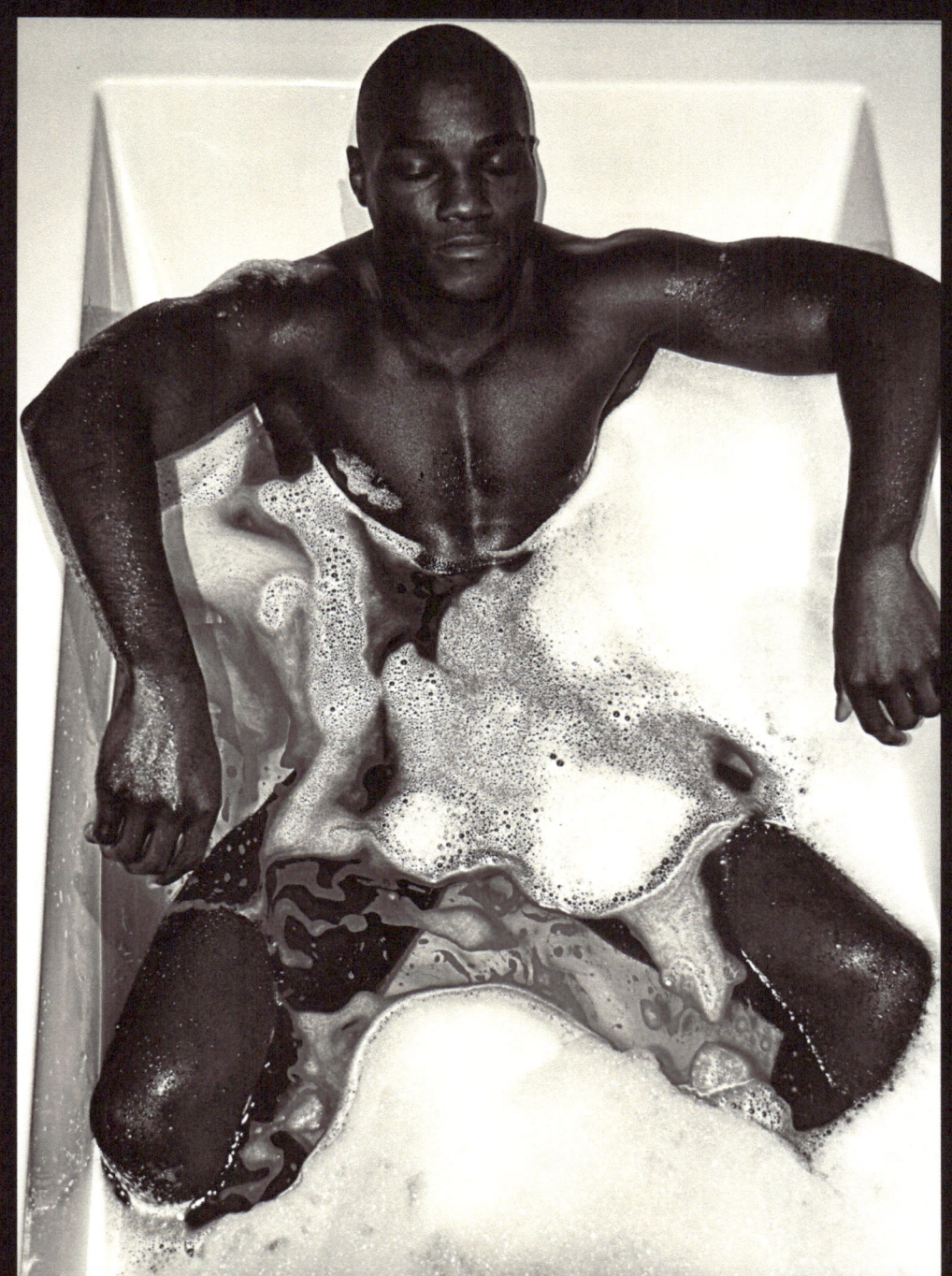

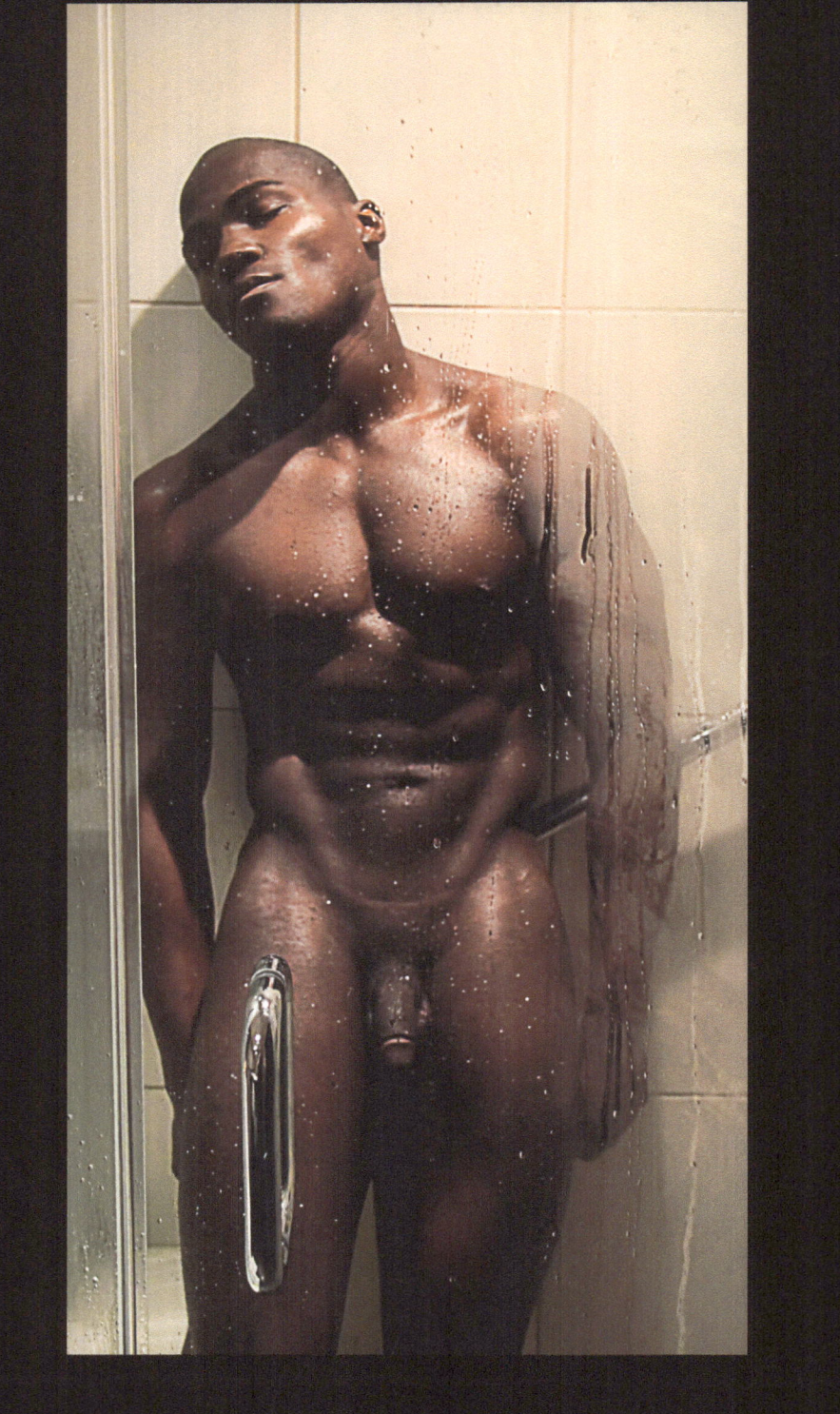

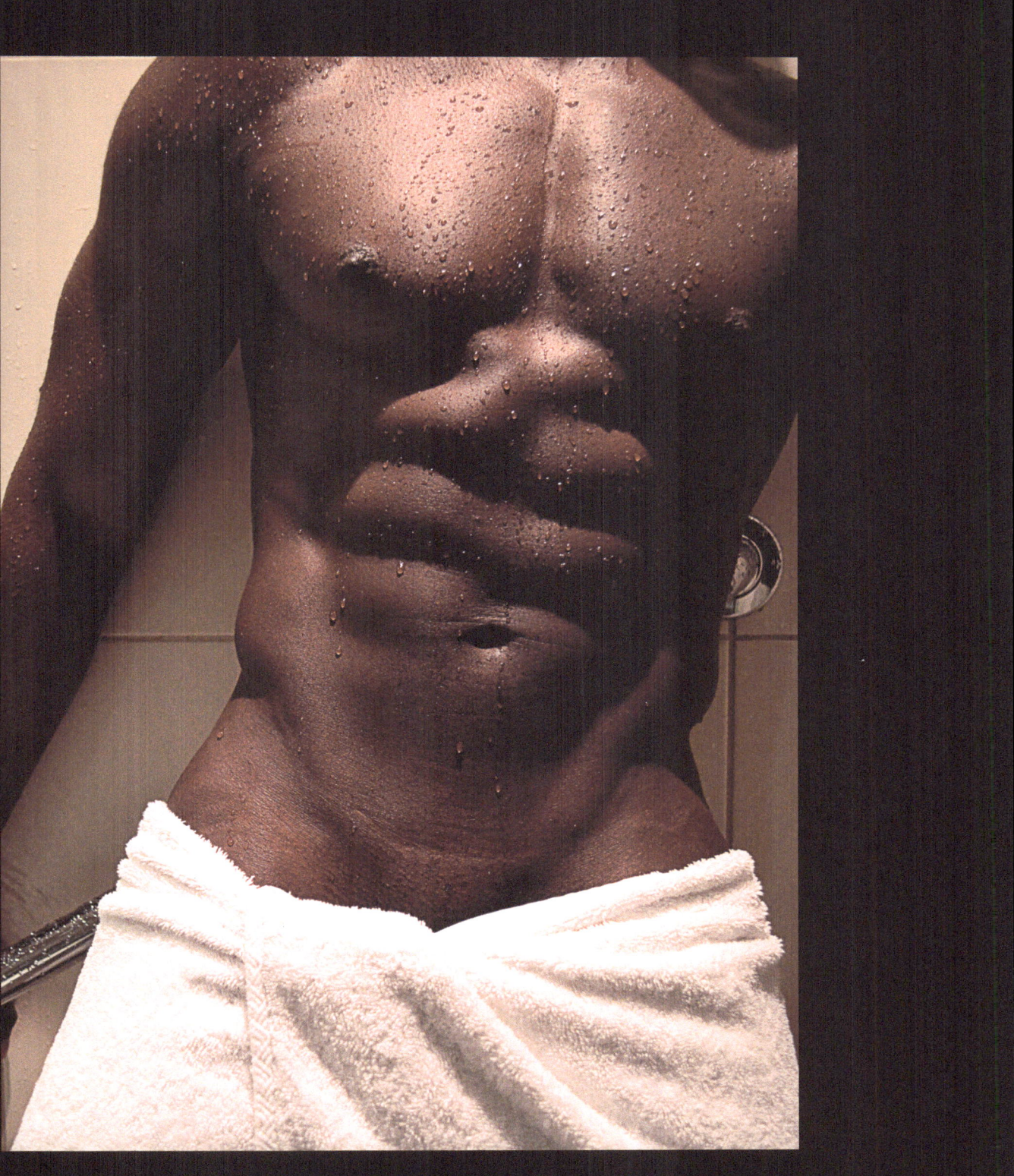

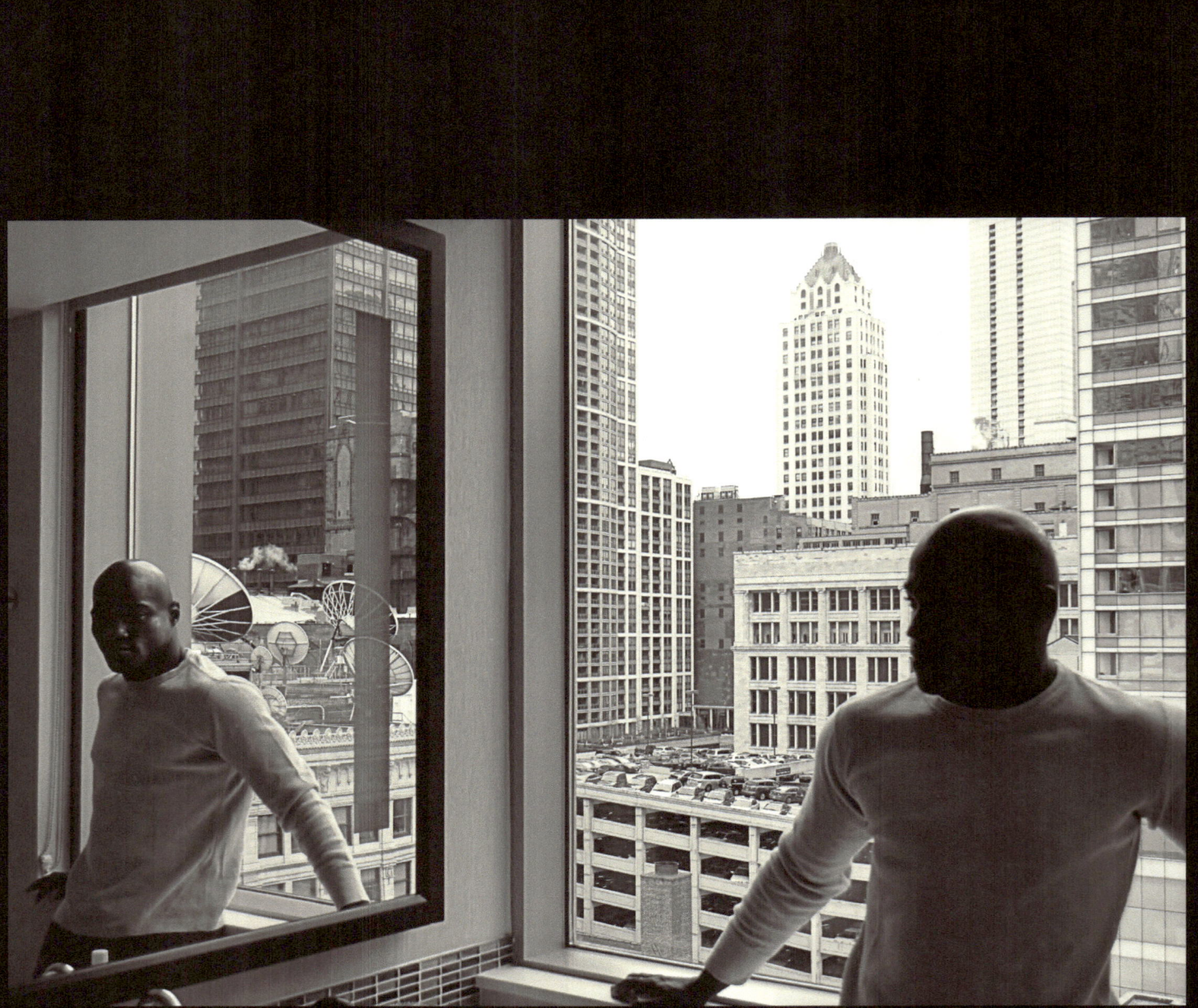

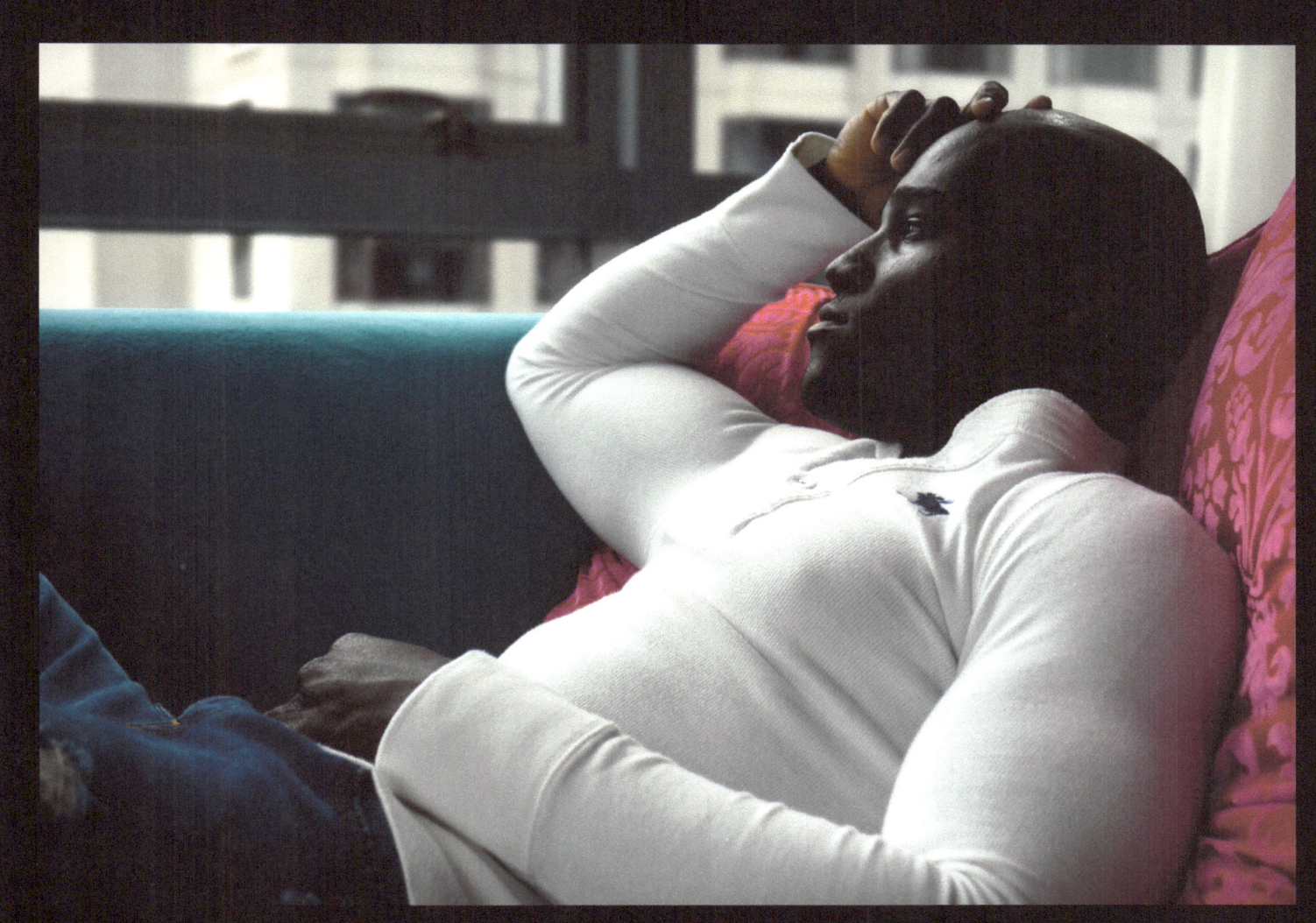

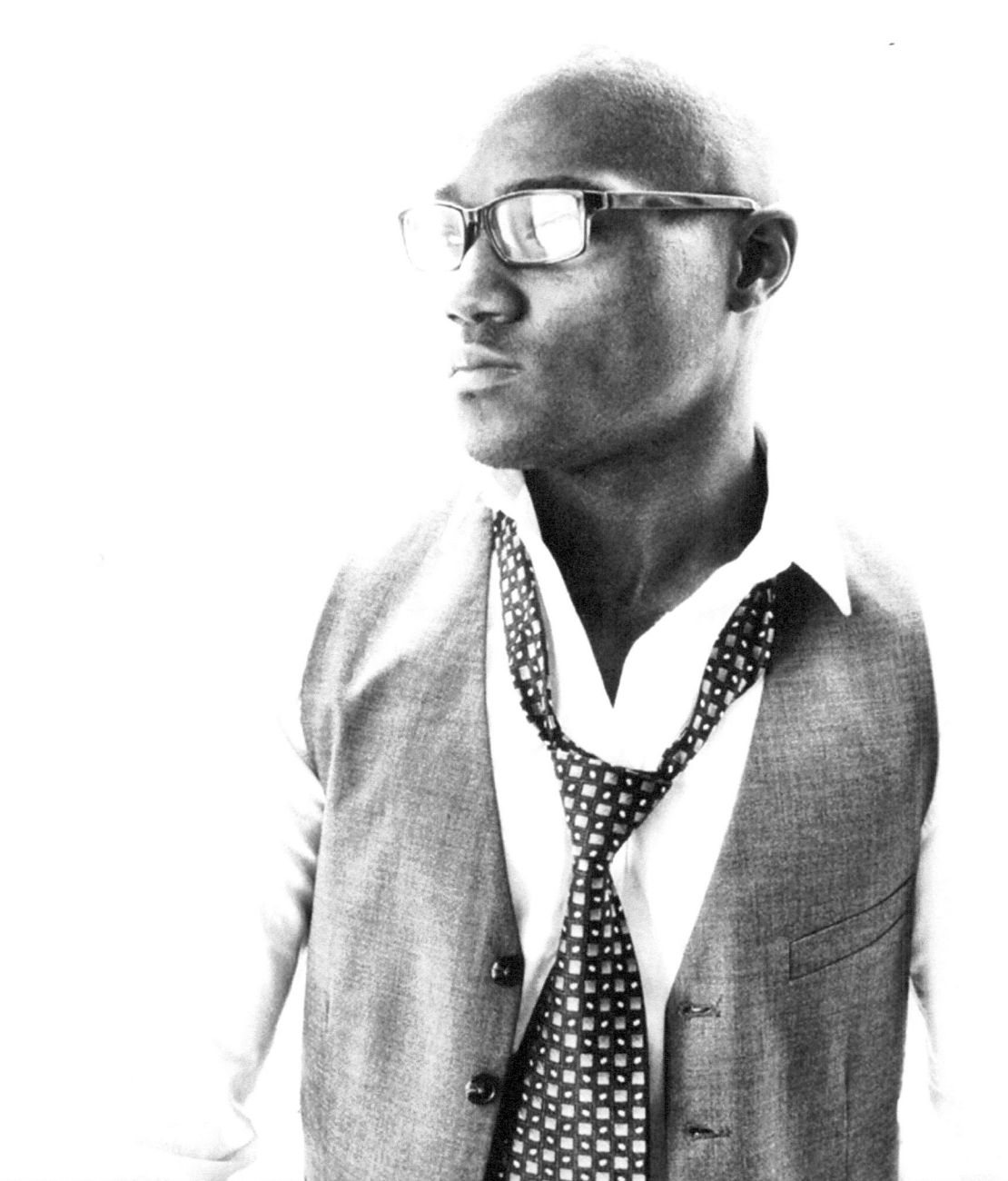

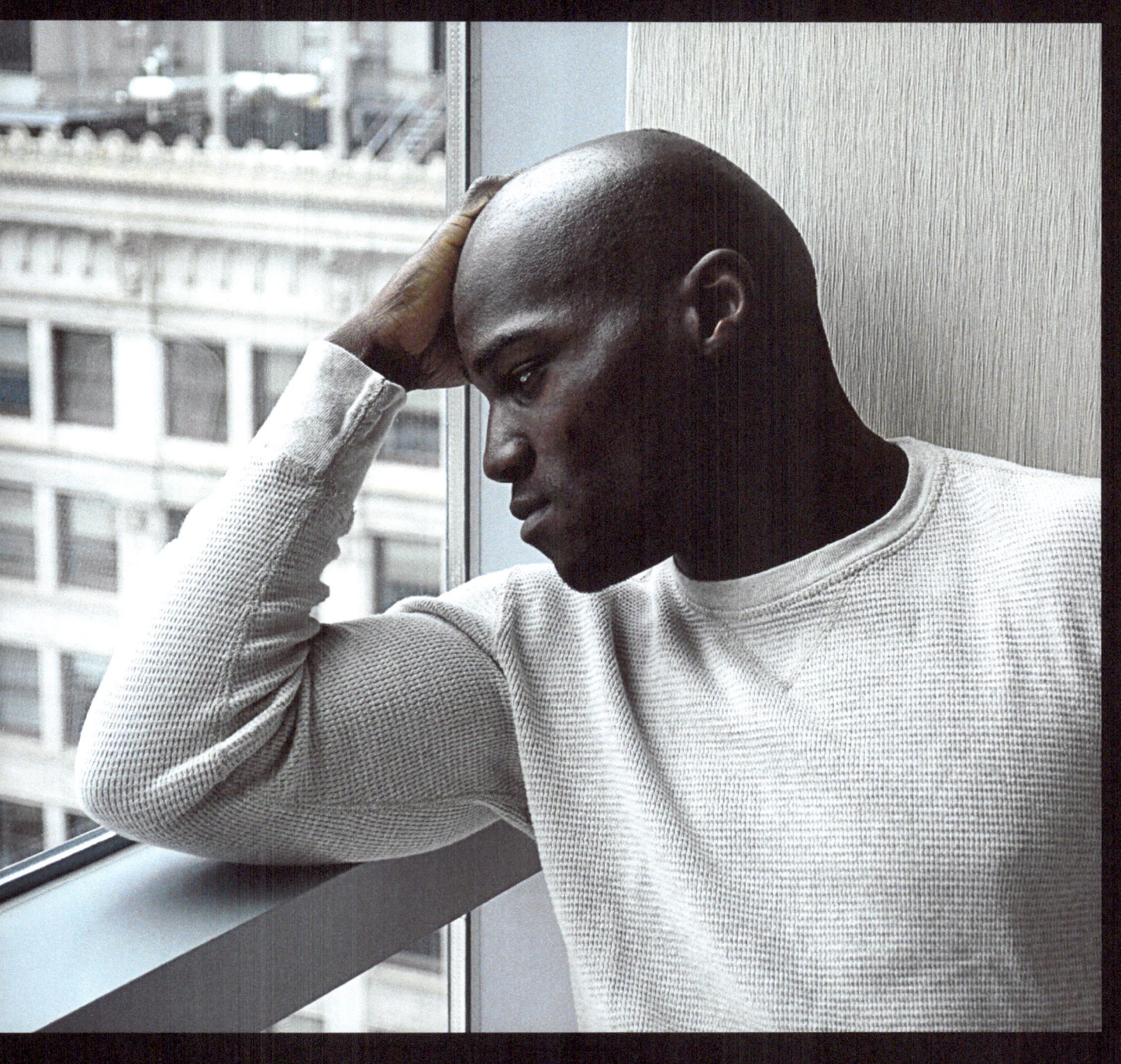

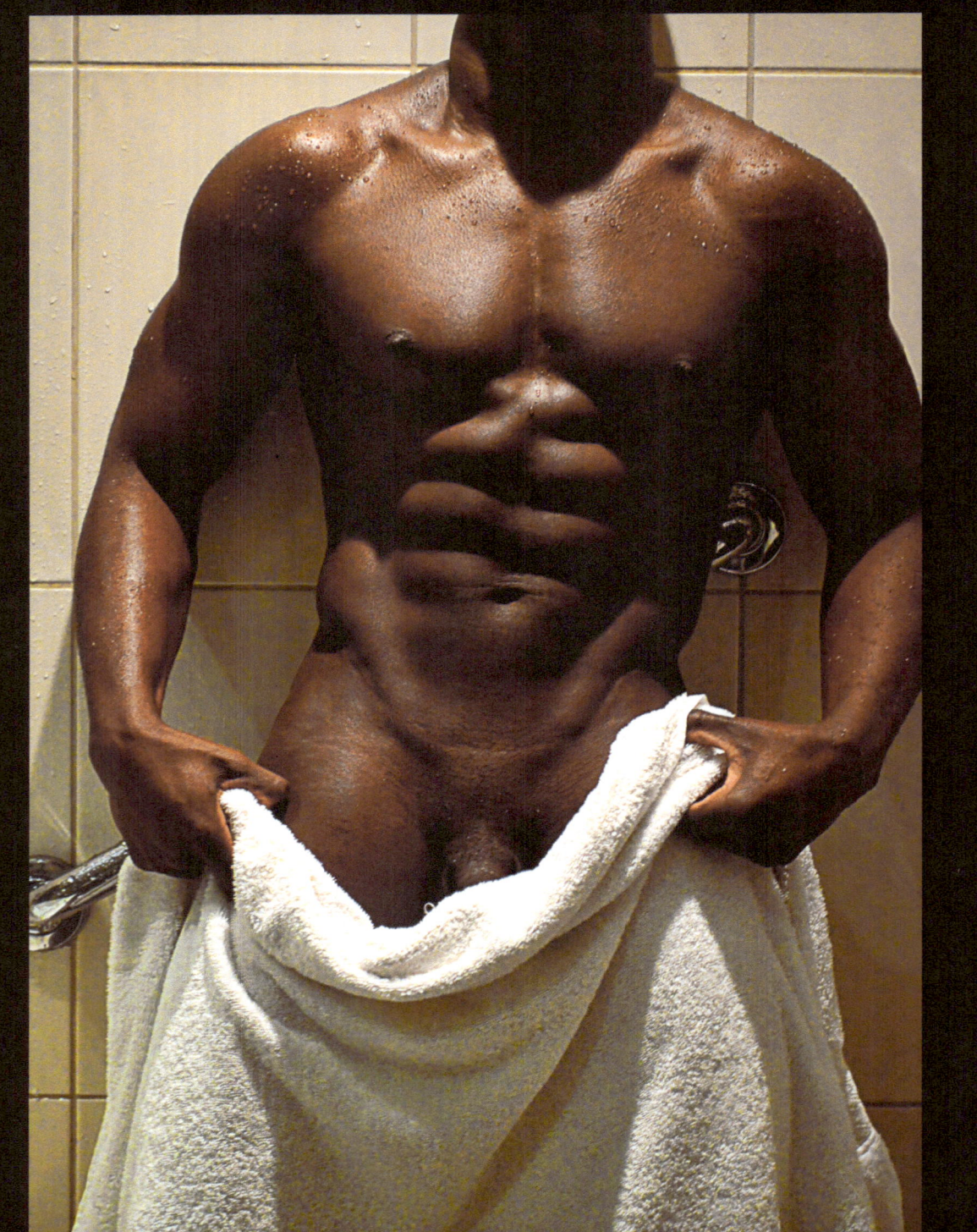

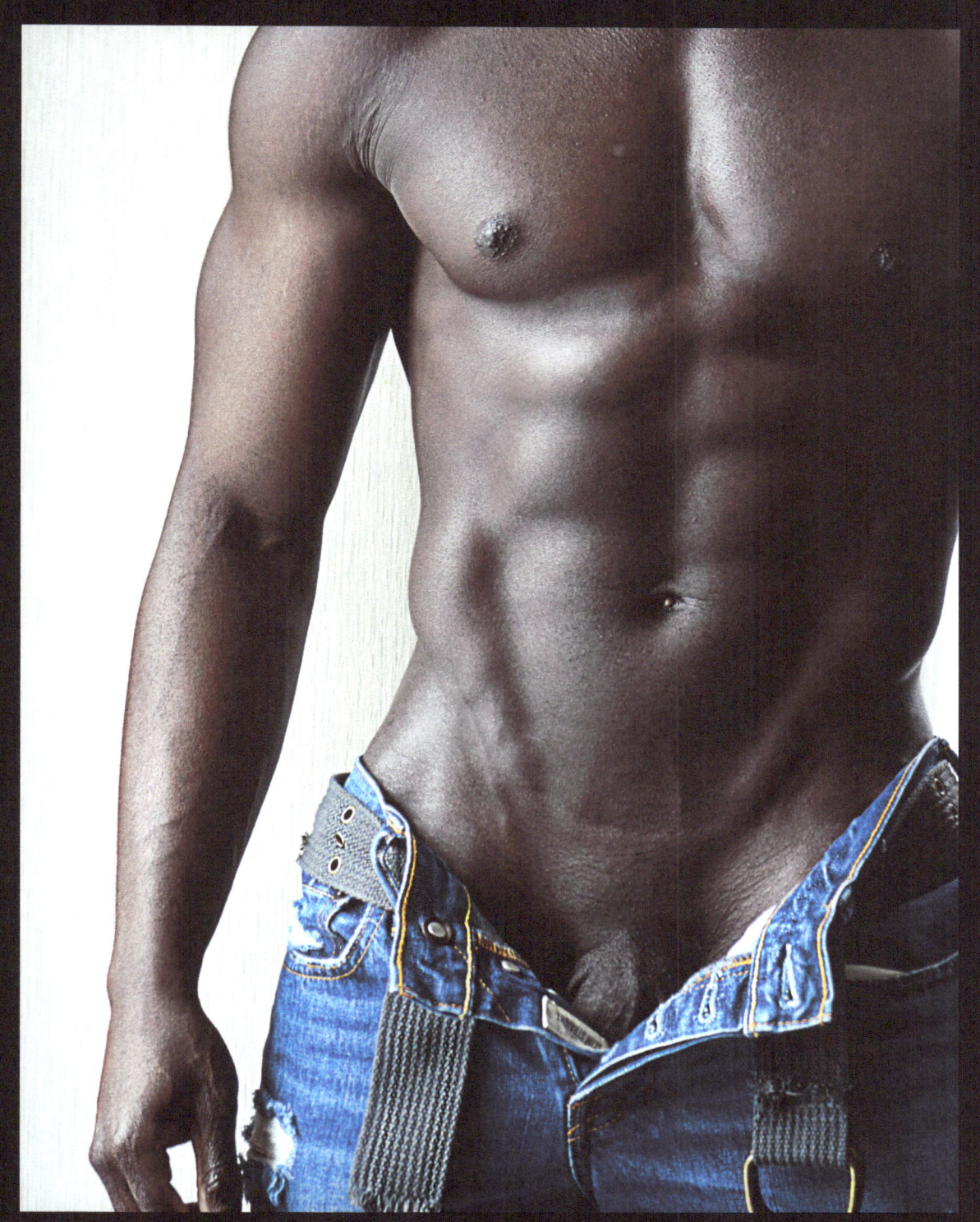

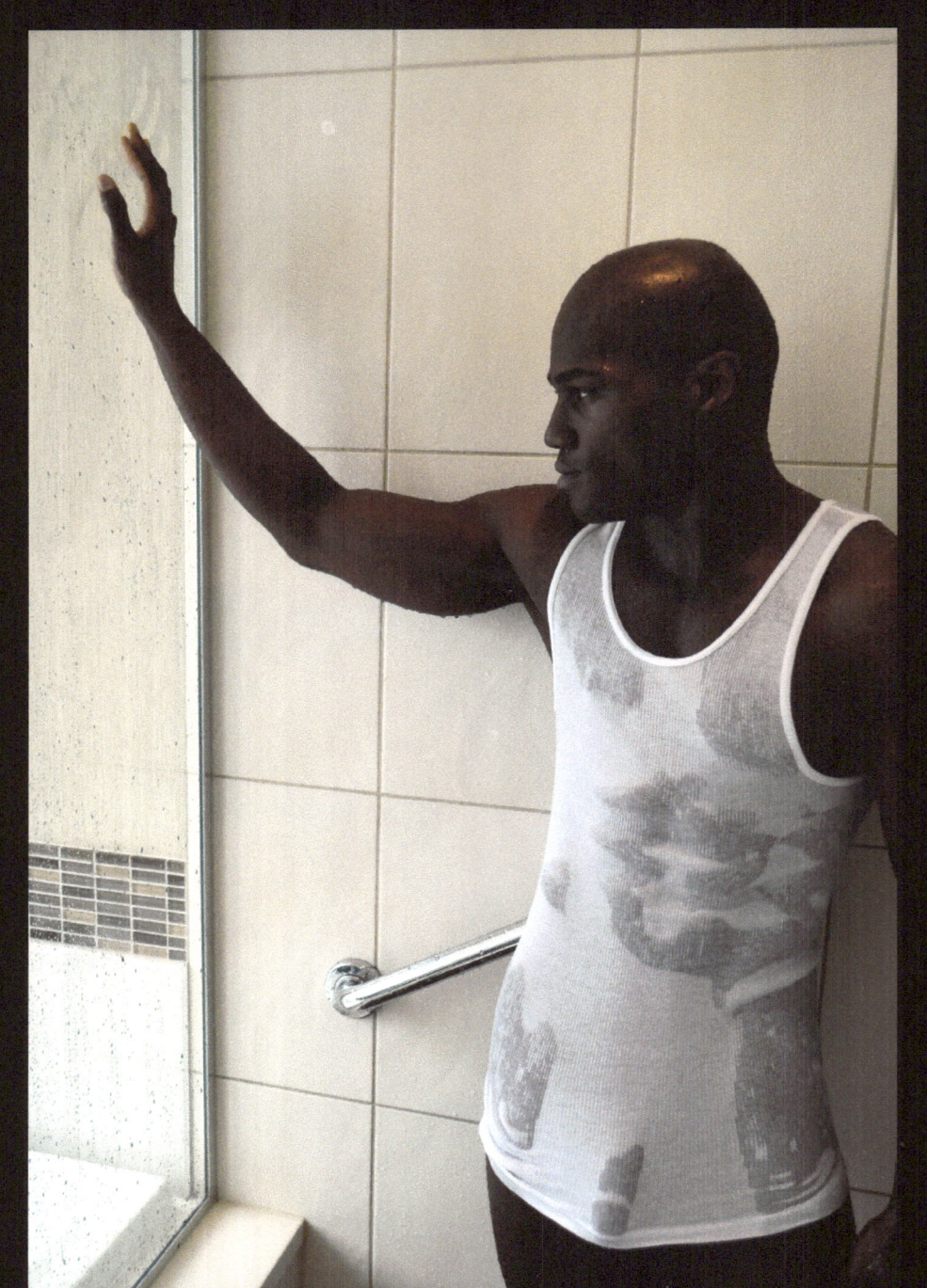

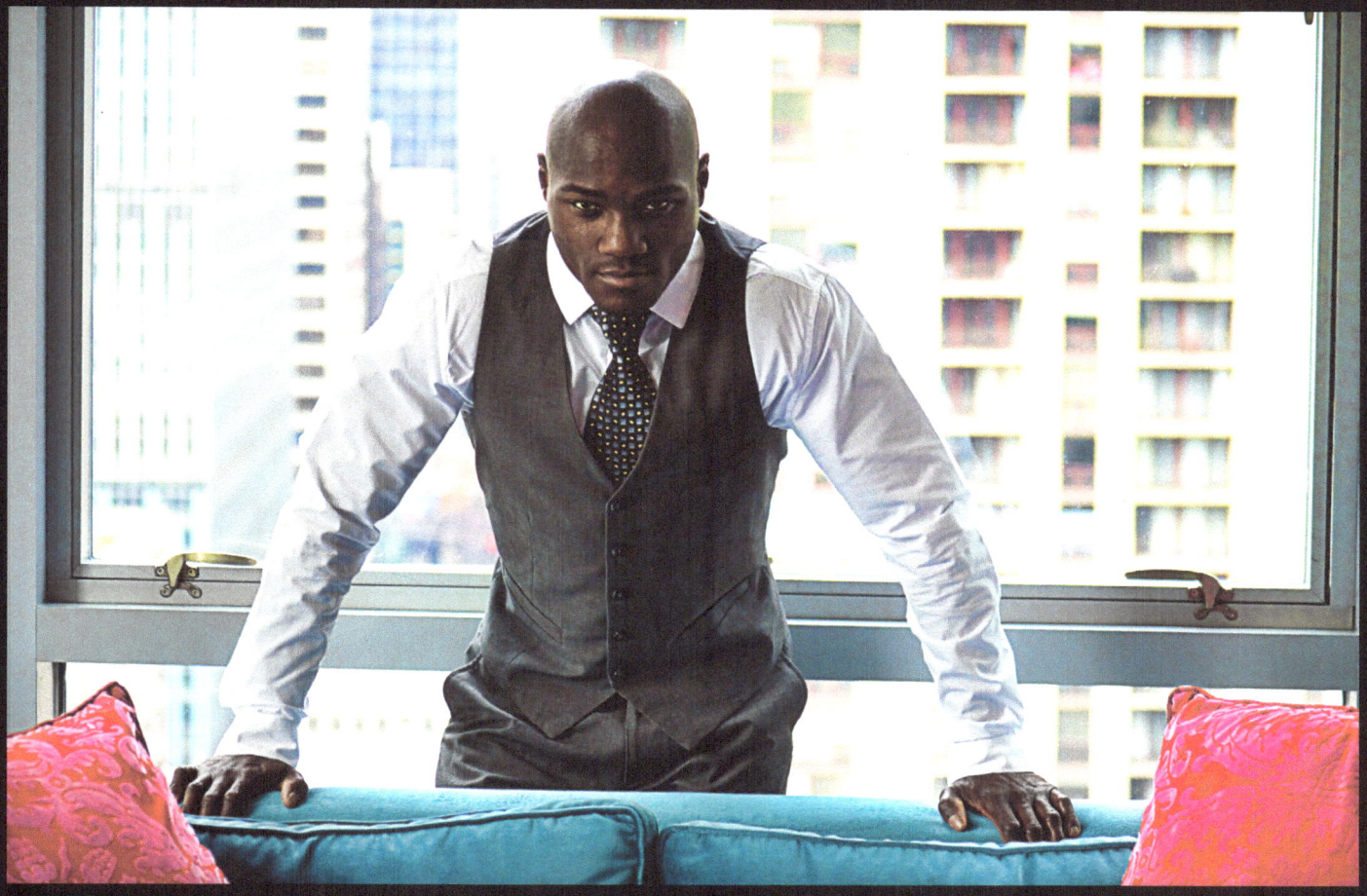

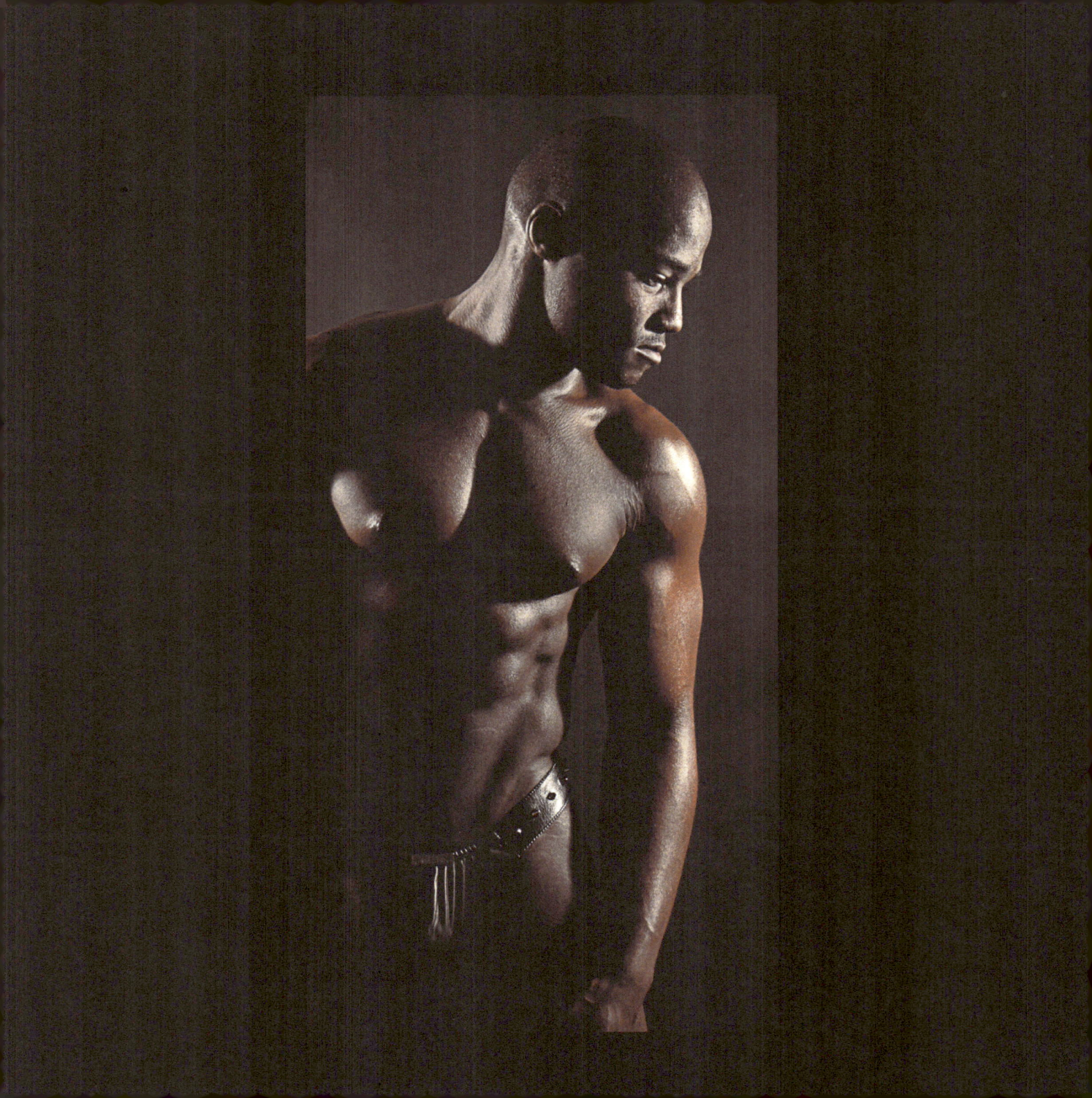

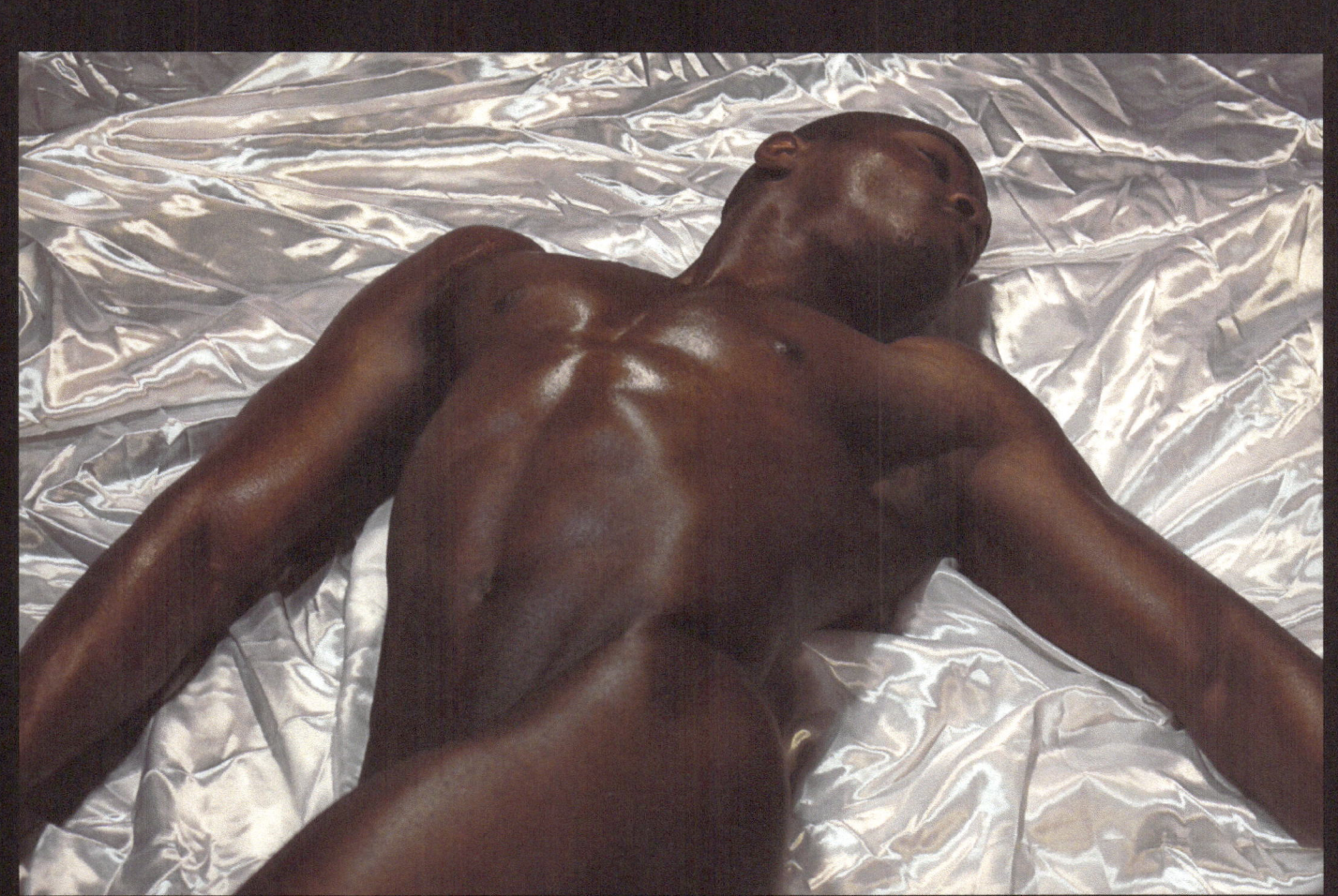

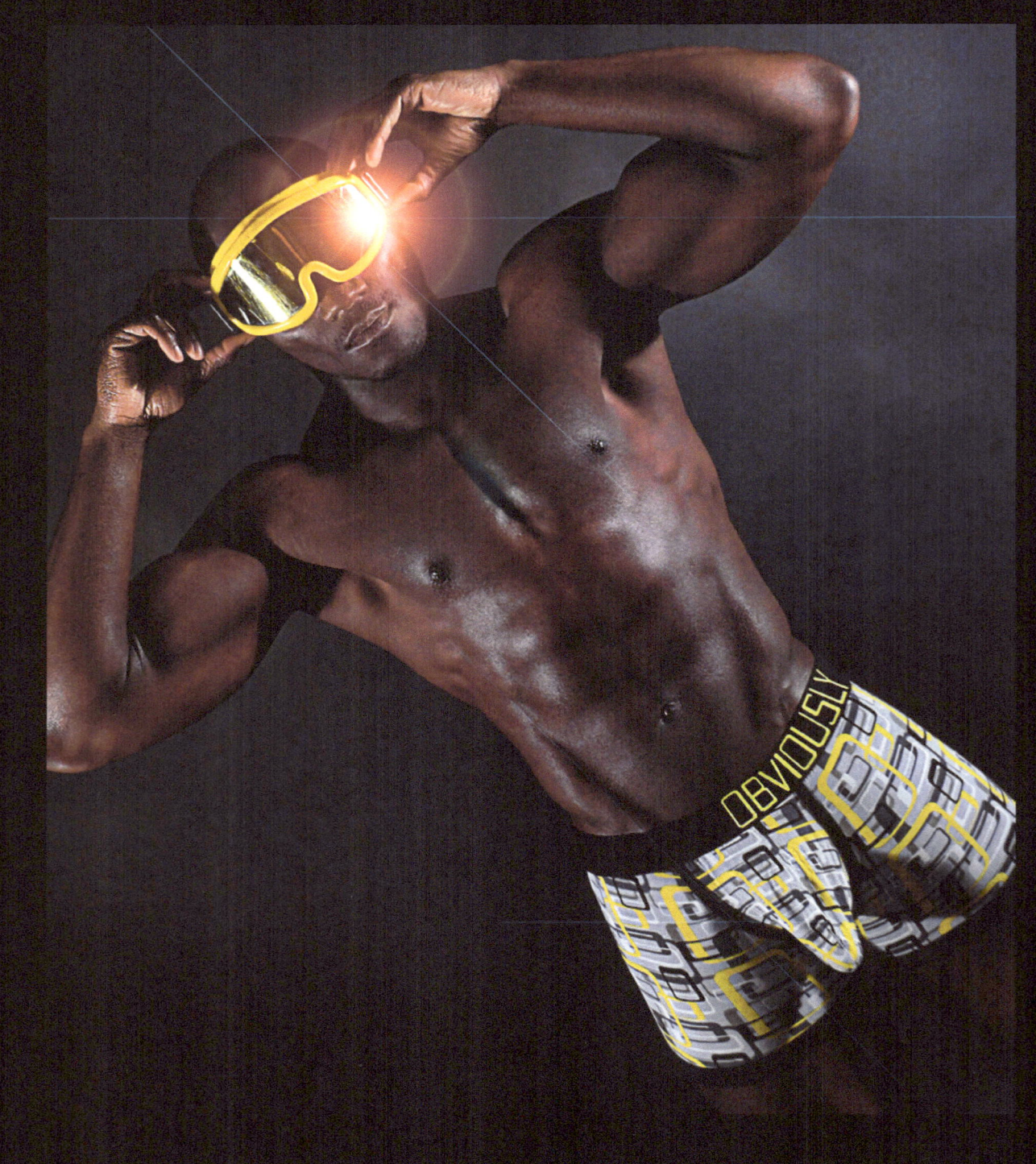

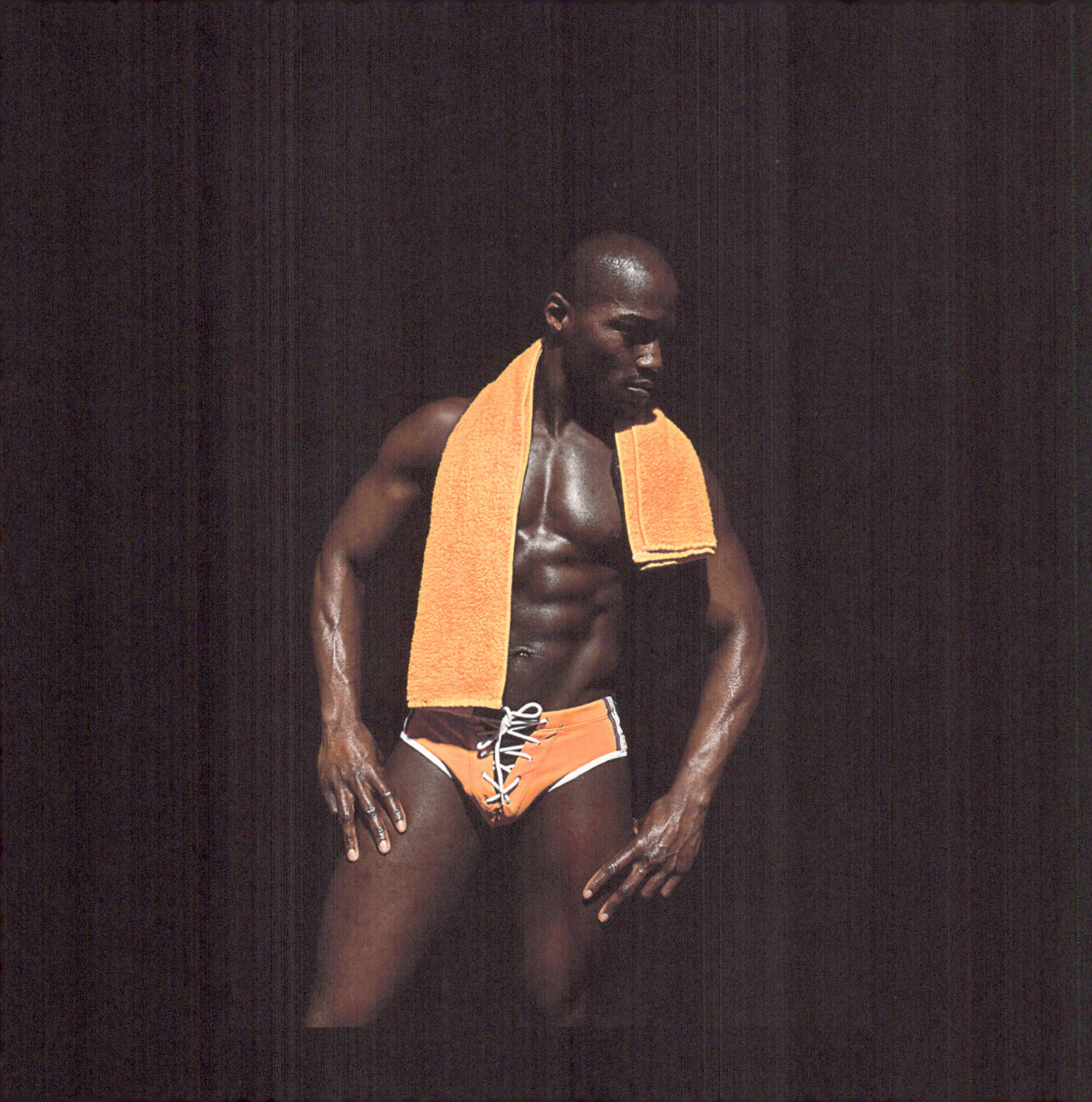

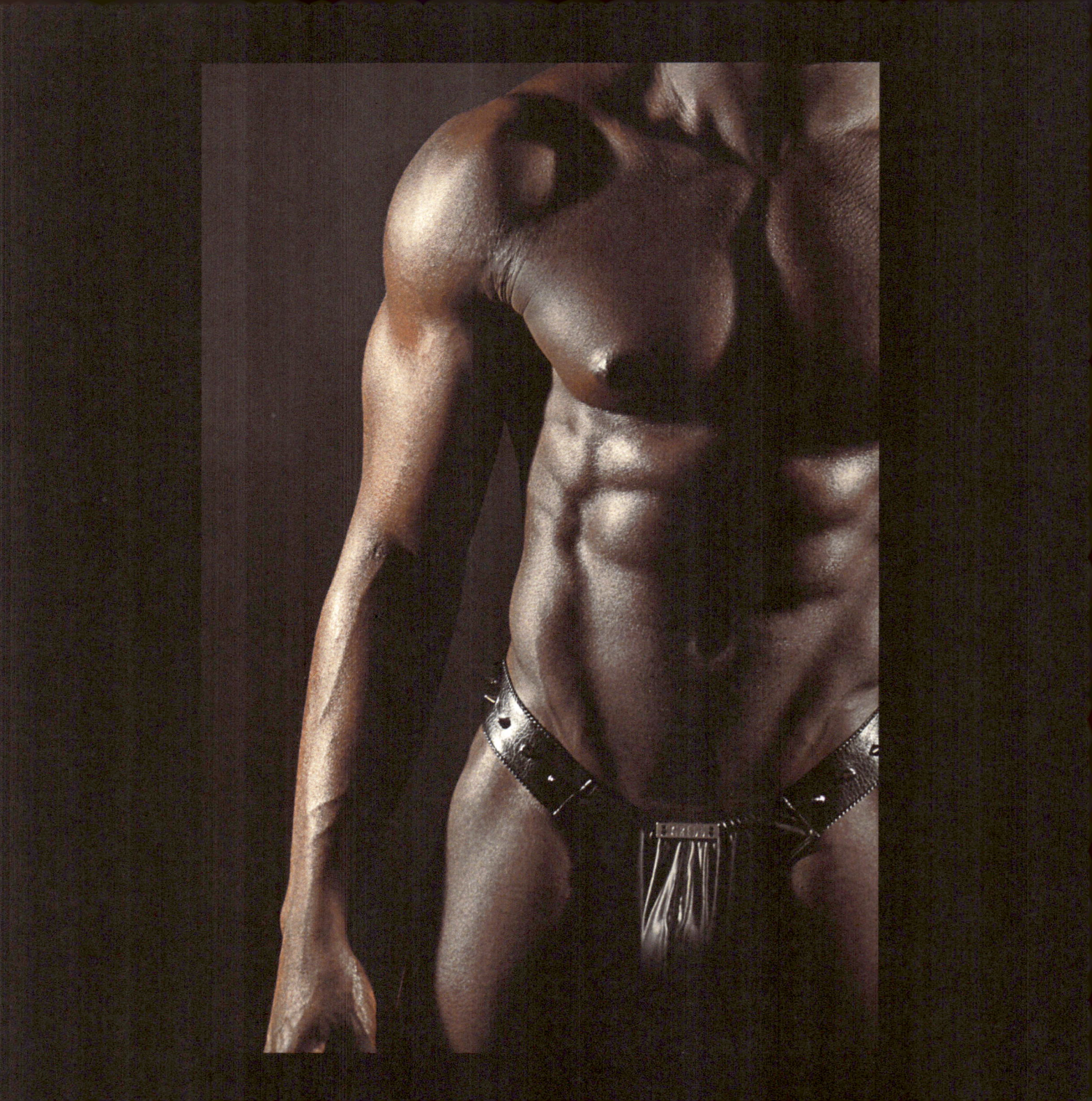

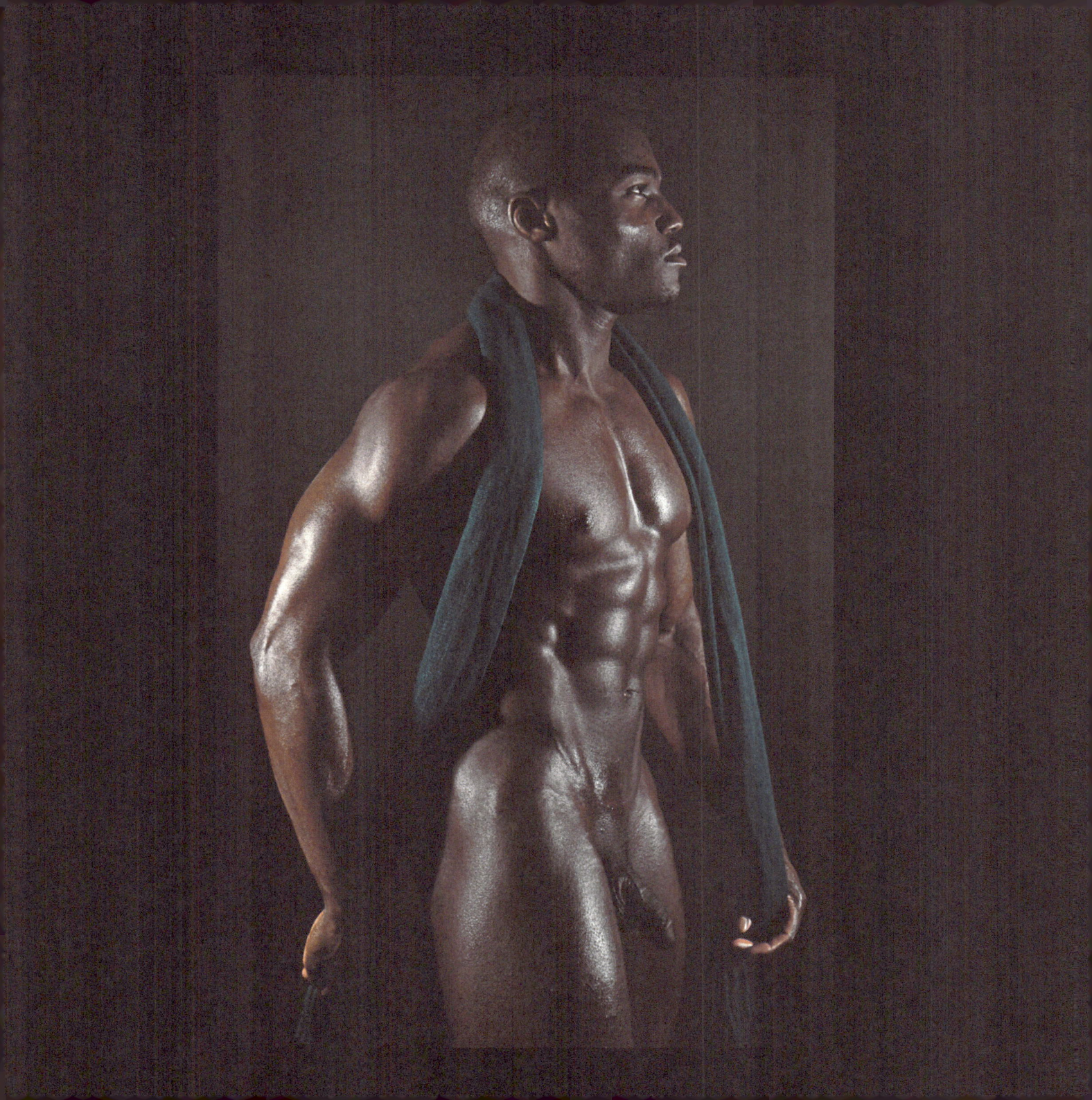

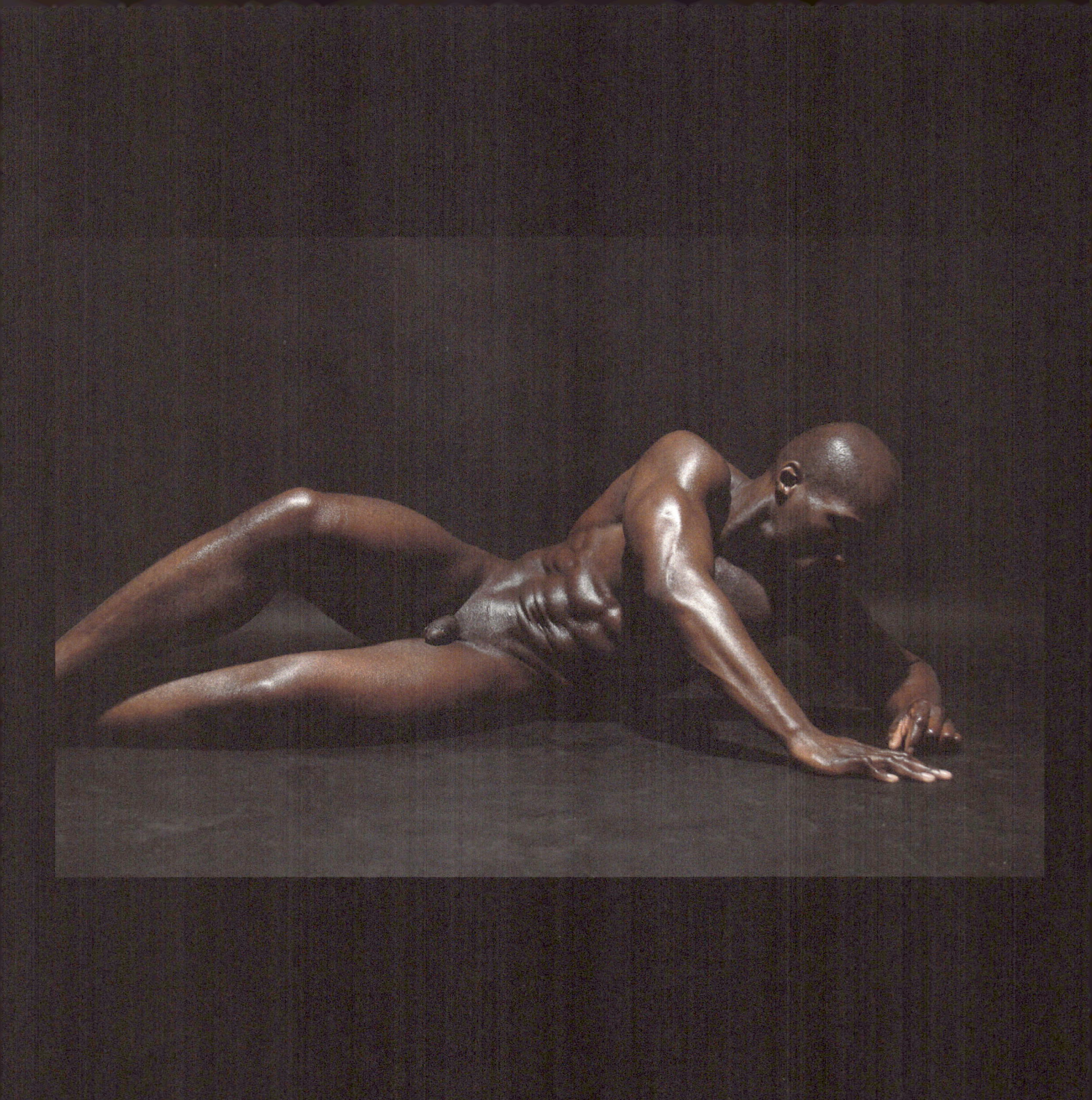

Stay tuned for volume 3...